WHAT OTHERS KNOW ABOUT THIS BOOK

I highly recommend this teaching by Kim Daniels. It is a book of revelation and insight concerning the deliverance ministry. Deliverance is an important ministry that requires apostolic insight, and Kim Daniels' insight into the spirit world is a gift from God. I particularly encourage the readers to draw from her insight into gates and gatekeepers. This book will help believers understand the depths of salvation and deliverance and give readers the ability to walk in greater anointing and discernment in helping set the captive free.

—APOSTLE JOHN ECKHARDT

Apostle Kim Daniels leads a "full speed ahead" attack on the enemy in *Clean House—Strong House*. This book is a priceless guide to effective ministry in spiritual warfare and deliverance. I highly recommend it to those "warriors" with a heart to set the captives free!

—DR. KINGSLEY A. FLETCHER
INTERNATIONAL SPEAKER AND AUTHOR
RESEARCH TRIANGLE PARK, NORTH CAROLINA

Are you desiring freedom in a way that you've never experienced before? Then *Clean House—Strong House* is for you! In this provocative book, Kim Daniels will show you not only how to receive your deliverance, but also how you can be an instrument in the deliverance of another. As you read this book, you will discover a purity and power reserved for those who want to live and walk in the fullness of Jesus Christ.

—ROD PARSLEY, FOUNDER AND PASTOR
WORLD HARVEST CHURCH
CEO, BREAKTHROUGH MEDIA MINISTRIES

Clean House Strong House

KIMBERLY DANIELS

CHARISMA HOUSE

CLEAN HOUSE—STRONG HOUSE by Kimberly Daniels
Published by Charisma House
Charisma Media/Charisma House Book Group
600 Rinehart Road
Lake Mary, Florida 32746
www.charismahouse.com

Unless otherwise noted, all Scripture quotations are from the New King James Version of the Bible. Copyright © 1979, 1980, 1982 by Thomas Nelson, Inc., publishers. Used by permission.

Scripture quotations marked AMP are from the Amplified Bible. Old Testament copyright © 1965, 1987 by the Zondervan Corporation. The Amplified New Testament copyright © 1954, 1958, 1987 by the Lockman Foundation. Used by permission.

Scripture quotations marked KJV are from the King James Version of the Bible.

Scripture quotations marked THE MESSAGE are from *The Message*, copyright © 1993, 1994, 1995. Used by permission of NavPress Publishing Group.

Names, places and identifying details with regard to stories in this book have been changed to protect the privacy of individuals who may have had similar experiences. The people referenced consist of composites of a number of people with similar issues, and the names and circumstances have been changed to protect their confidentiality. Any similarity between the names and stories of individuals described in this book to individuals known to readers is purely coincidental.

Cover design by Karen Grindley
Interior design by Sallie Traynor
Front and back cover photos by Reggie Anderson (www.reggiephotos4u.com)

Library of Congress Cataloging-in-Publication Data

Daniels, Kim.
 Clean house, strong house / Kim Daniels.
     p. cm.
 ISBN: 0-88419-964-9
 1. Spiritual warfare. I. Title.
 BV4509.5 .D24 2003
 235'.4—dc21
                                        2002151970
 ISBN-13: 978-0-88419-964-9
 E-book ISBN: 978-1-59979-498-3

12 13 14 15 16 — 19 18 17 16 15
Printed in the United States of America

I dedicate the contents of this work to my best friend, lover, protector, provider and "all that"—Jesus Christ! Lord, I present every word back to You as You have given them to me. I give You back the ministry You gave to me. I love You, Lord, and I thank You for opening the eyes of my understanding so that I would know the hope of my calling.

I would like to declare that I am nothing without You. I give You all the honor, glory and praise for helping me with this project.

Your baby, Kim

To the Reader

PRAISE THE LORD! By God's grace and mercy, He has anointed me to release the information in this book to His body. The Bible tells us that in all our getting, we must obtain understanding. In obtaining understanding, we must be careful "how we hear." Luke 8:17–18 says that there is nothing hidden that shall not be disclosed, nor anything secret that shall not be known and come out into the open. Be careful *how you listen.* For unto him who has spiritual knowledge will more be given, and from him who has not spiritual knowledge, even what he thinks he has will be taken away.

Based on this passage, there is a way to listen. In listening to the Word, we can obtain understanding in spiritual things or lose what we have to the mind of the flesh. I plead the blood of Jesus over your mind, in the name of Jesus. I pray that you will have an ear to hear (correctly) what God is saying to His body in the areas of warfare and deliverance.

I pray that you have enough of a foundation in the Word that what is in this book will not deplete you of what you already have. You cannot read this book with the mind of the flesh. The carnal mind cannot submit to the things of the Spirit.

I declare that the switch on the inside of you is flipped to the mind of the Spirit and the mind of the flesh is cut off. Ephesians 4:23 lets us know that we must be renewed in the spirit of our minds. This is my prayer for the readers of this book—that you will receive information and impartation that will destroy and bury every wrong thought about warfare and deliverance ministry. Also that your mind will be barricaded by the unadulterated truth and be renewed in the Spirit.

Before you go any further, I must explain the title of this book. *Clean House—Strong House* refers to having a strong house that is secured in the Lord vs. a house that has merely been swept clean, put in order and garnished. The phrase *clean house* is given in a negative sense. In order to really understand this, we must study three Greek words.

1. *Skoteinos*—opaque and full of darkness; to be a blockhead that cannot see the truth

2. *Skotos*—A shady, obscure darkness (producing swindlers, liars and deceivers)

3. *Skotia*—obscure, not clear, shady, lukewarm, dim, insipid, unable to distinguish

Our next step is to put scriptures with the meaning of these Greek words.

1. Luke 11:34 tells us that when the eye is evil, the body is full of darkness (*skoteinos*).

2. Luke 11:35 says that we, as believers, must be careful that the light in us be not darkness (*skotos*).

3. In John 1:5 we find that sometimes even when the light shines in the darkness (*skotia*), the darkness still does not comprehend it.

Matthew 12:43–44 puts the icing on the cake when it says that when an unclean spirit goes out of a man (after we are delivered), it seeks dry places. When the spirit cannot find a dry place, it seeks a familiar place (the person that it has once abided in). When it finds the house (body) of that person swept clean, it reenters with seven other spirits (more wicked than the one that left). Although the darkness had been swept out of this house, allowing the light to be exposed, the darkness reentered—this time with seven times more darkness and obscurity.

It is very clear, based on these scriptures and the interpretation of the key Greek words emphasized, that not only can a Christian have a demon, but even though the evil is swept out of his life, and the light exposed, the darkness can return and he can become seven times worse than before he was saved and delivered.

These three Greek words warn us that after we have obtained light, we must be careful that it "be not darkness." What are the manifestations of our light being darkness?

- Operating in shady or obscure ways in ministry, even in dealing with people on an everyday basis (Luke 11:35).

- Walking in a spirit of lukewarmness. The lukewarm church was the only one that God did not have a good thing to say about when He addressed the seven churches in the Book of Revelation (Rev. 3:16).

- Exhibiting or showing stubbornness in doctrine or an ungodly drive to be *religiously right* coupled with an "unteachable spirit." This promotes darkness and hinders new truths. It leads to a shipwreck of faith and a warfare that is not good (1 Tim. 1:18–20; 2 Tim. 2:17–18).

- Being a breeding ground for carnality with no spiritual discipline in the areas of what is holy and what is common (Lev. 10:10).

To sum up the meaning of the title and the vision of this

work, God is saying to the church of the twenty-first century that it is time to separate ourselves from the things in the world that would contaminate our minds and block us from the truth. This is pertinent in our endeavor to manifest ourselves (to all of creation) as the true sons of God. We must avoid and renounce that which will make us operate in obscurity and under the mantle of shadiness.

The world must be able to distinguish the difference between us and all others who come in the name of God. If we do not take heed to this word and take the measures necessary to maintain our deliverance, the same things that we have been delivered from will draw to the *skotia* in us and make us seven times worse.

The following scriptures are in support of the truth I speak:

> For it is impossible for those who were once enlightened, and *have tasted* of the heavenly gift, and *were made partakers* of the *Holy Ghost,* and *have tasted* the good word of God, and the powers of the world to come, *if they shall fall away,* to renew them again unto repentance; seeing they crucify to themselves the Son of God afresh, and put him to an open shame.
>
> —Hebrews 6:4–7, KJV, emphasis added

> If it were possible, they shall deceive the very elect.
>
> —Matthew 24:24, KJV

The word *deceive* is *planao* in the Greek, and it means "to cause to roam from safety and truth." It literally means to be moved from the *light* of the truth to the darkness of deception.

Remember that we are praying for revival. We need revival *in us,* and we desire to see souls revived from the kingdom of darkness into His "marvelous light" (1 Pet. 2:9). The word *marvelous* is *thaumastos,* and it means "a light to be admired and desired." They that come in must see the light.

PREACHERS

Preacher, if you are preaching that a Christian cannot have a demon or that once a person is saved he is always saved, get on your knees and repent quickly! We love you, but we hate a pretty gospel! Jesus did not preach a pretty gospel, and we cannot do so.

Paul, to me, was one of the least religious of the apostles. He did not actually walk, sleep and eat with the Master as the others did. He was raised by the devil far away from Christ. When he came into his ministry, he was not bound by the status quo or the fashion of the church.

His walk was by faith…"the just shall live by faith" (Heb. 10:38)!

I pray a Paulean anointing upon you that you will come out of the ministry of pleasing man into the ministry of the full gospel. It is not about *if your denomination does it or if your peers are doing it.*

Join me and *do what Jesus did.* Deliverance is not an option—it is the ministry of Jesus Christ! Is your house swept clean, set in order and decorated? Are your church programs uninterruptible, and do they flow with such a beautiful precision that even the Holy Ghost Himself cannot intervene? We can be in so much religious order that we are out of order in God.

Demons are seeking places that proclaim Jesus but are so beautifully and carnally decorated that God could not move if He wanted to. Sometimes the Lord has to mess up our clean house and make it a strong house so that He can get the glory.

Look at this scripture:

> For thus saith the LORD of hosts; Yet once, it is a little while, and I will shake the heavens, and the earth, and the sea, and the dry land; and I will shake all the nations, and the desire of all nations shall come: and I will fill this house with glory, saith the LORD of hosts.
>
> The silver is mine, and the gold is mine, saith the LORD

of hosts. The glory of the latter house shall be greater than
of the former, saith the LORD of hosts: and in this place will
I give peace, saith the LORD of hosts.

—HAGGAI 2:6–9, KJV

The glory of the latter house will be greater. But the Lord has
declared there will be a shaking first. This shaking will ignite
order—God's order! But it will tear down the demonic deception of order that has set itself (beautifully) in the house of God
to hinder the true glory. The wealth of the wicked is stored up
for the just, but God has to shake some things first.

True Paulean anointing prompts us to know Him! This
knowing is not just in the power of His resurrection, but in the
fellowship of His suffering. Preacher, if you want to reign with
Him as a part of the priesthood, you must suffer with Him in the
ministry that He did most.

The work of deliverance and warfare was an everyday walk
for Jesus. He walked it out in victory. The purpose of this book
is that this ministry will not be such a strange thing. Familiarize
yourself with the ministry of Jesus Christ!

I am not saying that deliverance is all that we should do, but
I am saying Jesus said that when we are not with Him in this
ministry, we are against Him (Matt. 12:30). We scatter when we
are called to gather. Allow the Holy Spirit to mess up your *clean
house* and to make it a *strong house!*

> But when the unclean spirit has gone out of a man, it
> roams through dry [arid] places in search of rest, but it
> does not find any. Then it says, I will go back to my house
> from which I came out. And when it arrives, it finds the
> place unoccupied, swept, put in order, and decorated.
>
> Then it goes and brings with it seven other spirits more
> wicked than itself, and they go in and make their home
> there. And the last condition of that man becomes worse
> than the first. So also shall it be with this wicked generation.
>
> —MATTHEW 12:43–45, AMP

Contents

Foreword

THE BIBLE OFFERS us a curious bit of trivia about one of Jesus' followers, Mary Magdalene, in Luke 8:2. The Gospel account describes her as a woman "out of whom had come seven demons." That's not exactly how any of us would want to be described, but Mary's deliverance from these evil spirits must have made quite an impact on her and those who knew her. I wonder if Luke was watching the scene when Jesus cast these devils out of Mary one by one. If Luke ever had doubted the power of God before, watching that dramatic deliverance session would have made a believer out of him!

Mary's experience reminds me that the ministry of deliverance is not just something Jesus does for wild-eyed demoniacs who hang around in graveyards and talk to themselves. Deliverance is for those who follow Jesus closely. In fact, if we really want to be intimate with Jesus, then we should expect that He will have to cast the darkness out of us. Many of us who love the Lord—even those in full-time ministry—still battle with life-controlling addictions, sinful tendencies or occult bondage that we try to hide under our respectable religious masks. We can't blame our problems on the devil, but all of us need Jesus to free us from the root causes of our sin.

For years Christians have argued back and forth about whether it is possible for a born-again believer to have a demon. After all, how can a devil live comfortably alongside the Holy Spirit? I used to ask that question too—until one day in 1988 when two pastors cast a demon out of me. What happened that day did not match my theology, but I could not discount the experience.

I asked these two men to pray with me because I was struggling with a recurring habit that brought a great deal of guilt and shame into my life. As we talked about my past, we identified some hurtful experiences from my childhood that obviously had created an opportunity for the devil to gain a foothold. As we talked and prayed together, I began to sob—simply because I had never shared this pain or embarrassment with anyone before.

Suddenly I realized that my hands were becoming contorted. A strange sensation of numbness moved into my arms and into my chest. Within a few more moments it had spread all the way to my face. I felt as if my entire upper torso were paralyzed. I could barely even move my mouth to speak. The two pastors recognized immediately that this was a manifestation of a demonic spirit, and they gently laid me on the floor and began praying more aggressively.

One of the pastors began to command the spirit to come out. Nothing happened for a while, and the tightness in my face and chest actually began to feel painful. It was almost as if an invisible octopus were squeezing me in a vice grip. My fists were clinched tight, my mouth was dry, and the skin on my face felt like leather. Yet somehow I sensed a peace in my heart—because I knew God was performing a miracle.

"Come out of him! In the name of Jesus!" one of the pastors shouted. After a few minutes I began to sense an invisible presence moving up from my abdomen, into my chest and toward my head. I didn't say anything, but the numbness and tightness began to weaken. Within about fifteen minutes it was all over. I was free.

From that point in my Christian life, I came to understand that there are times when Jesus can and will perform a miracle of deliverance to liberate us from the devil's power. We don't have to focus on it, and we certainly shouldn't prescribe deliverance as the answer to every problem. But neither should we ever rule it out. Today, many Christians are living in a continual state of defeat because someone told them that believers never need deliverance. The devil loves that lie, because it gives him more room to hide in the church!

I am so glad Jesus has raised up voices today to remind us that deliverance is for today and that it is available to God's people. Kim Daniels, like Mary Magdalene, knows the power of deliverance because Jesus has touched her so powerfully. And because of the anointing of the Holy Spirit on her life, she and her husband, Ardell, have seen many people completely delivered from the chains of occult bondage, sexual perversion, religious deception and ancestral curses. Kim is reminding us that Jesus wants His church to be pure—inside and out.

I pray that *Clean House—Strong House* will help you clean out your own life so that you can be a tool in the Lord's hands to bring deliverance to many others.

—J. Lee Grady, Editor
Charisma Magazine

Chapter 1

The New Birth

L ATE ONE NIGHT a prominent leader among the Jews visited Jesus. He had heard much about Jesus, and no doubt he had even listened to Jesus as He taught in Jerusalem. But he had questions for Jesus—questions he didn't dare ask in front of his Pharisee peers. Probably a lot of people even today would like to ask Jesus the same questions.

Nicodemus began by saying, "Rabbi, we all know you're a teacher straight from God. No one could do all the God-pointing, God-revealing acts you do if God weren't in on it" (John 3:2, THE MESSAGE). Obviously, he didn't want to offend Jesus with his questions, so he let Jesus know that he recognized Jesus was doing things that could only be done by someone connected somehow with God Himself.

Jesus, who already knew the questions within Nicodemus's heart, got right to the point: "You're absolutely right," He responded to Nicodemus. Then He hit the target by saying, "Take it from me: Unless a person is born from above, it's not possible to see what I'm pointing to—to God's kingdom" (v. 3, THE MESSAGE).

That was it! That's the very reason Nicodemus came quietly at night to see Jesus. That was his question! Quickly he responded back to Jesus: "How can anyone...be born who has already been born and grown up? You can't re-enter your mother's womb and be born again. What are you saying with this 'born-from-above' talk?" (v. 4, The Message).

If you keep reading in John 3, you will discover that Jesus clearly explained this new birth about which He spoke to Nicodemus. I want to help you answer that question in this chapter as I explain the process of being born again. I want to show you how to walk out of the darkness of a life without Jesus into the marvelous light of His salvation.

John 8:36 says, "Therefore if the Son makes you free, you shall be free indeed." Nicodemus had a longing in his heart to experience that freedom—but he didn't understand how to make it happen. This chapter will open the door to an understanding of how to be born again. Through the process of the new birth we move from darkness into light, from sin to salvation, from the bondage of the enemy to the delivering power of Jesus Christ. Making that transition from darkness to light will make you "free indeed."

To help you understand this process, I will use the comparison of a military prisoner of war who has been released. Prisoners of war endure terrible bondage during their captivity. Many die as prisoners due to the inhumane treatment they receive. What wonderful freedom they experience when they are set free from that captivity and are returned to their homes and families. Just as POWs are released from the ravages of war, so too the person who accepts Jesus as personal Savior is released from extreme circumstances to enter into the light of Jesus Christ.

During their captivity, POWs are often deprived of three things: space, light and food. In this first chapter you will see how satan deprives those in captivity to sin of these same three spiritual dynamics.

DEPRIVATION OF SPACE

Prisoners of war are given very limited living space—often merely a hole in the ground or a tiny, cramped cell. Can you imagine having to sit day after agonizing day in a hole so small that you could hardly straighten your legs? Once released from those cramped quarters, no doubt you would be very protective of the space you finally have. You may even be unapproachable because of the fear of allowing others in your space.

Life can crowd a person to the point of suffocation, and that person may not understand why. Satan loves to crowd people and give them limited living spaces. He knows that Jesus promised each of His children abundant life (John 10:10). The enemy crowds his captives with oppressing lifestyles, addictions, bondages and emotions from which they have no means of escape.

But Jesus came to set the captives free. (See Isaiah 61:1–3.) When people are set free from the oppression of the enemy, they enter a process of renewal. Just as a POW must be reacclimated to living free, the new believer must learn to live free in Christ. In 2 Corinthians 5:17 we read, "Therefore, if anyone is in Christ, he is a new creation; old things have passed away; behold, all things *have become new*" (emphasis added). The key words in this verse are "have become new." Another way to say it would be, "All things *are becoming* new." It is a process! The process of becoming new involves several steps:

- *Reconciliation*—man's reconnection with God

- *Restoration*—renovation of the soul (mind)

- *Transformation*—an outward change that is visible to the natural eye

The prerequisites of *reconnection, restoration* and *transformation* begin the process of coming into the light. Get connected with God, and allow Him to tear down your own will and rebuild His will for your life. Once the renovation has taken place, be willing to walk in the change. Many are allergic to change. The spirits of the world follow us, trying to get us to keep things as they were before salvation. There is a constant struggle with change.

When you understand the process, it will be easier to come into the light. The purpose of the process is to cause a series of actions that will bring about results. Each action will move us further along in the process of the new birth.

DEPRIVATION OF LIGHT

POWs are also denied the benefits of light. Day after day, year after year, they are confined to dark cells where the light of day never appears. When they emerge from their dark prison cells, they must go through a gradual transitioning into the light. Extreme light would be damaging to the eyes immediately.

Jesus came to deliver us from the darkness of sin. In the Book of Psalms we read:

> Then they cried out to the LORD in their trouble, and He saved them out of their distresses. He brought them out of darkness and the shadow of death, and broke their chains in pieces.
>
> —PSALM 107:13–14

When people come out of dark situations like drug addiction, the occult and homosexuality, it is a process. A man who has been filled with hatred must learn to love all people, a homosexual has to learn to be a man again, and a drug addict must learn to depend only on God.

Luke 8:16 is such a powerful evangelistic word. It tells us that the saints who are in God should allow His light to be seen so that "those who enter may see the light." Seeing this light is a process. We need people with the heart of the Father who are willing to mentor and raise up the new generation of saints who are coming into His light. If we are overbearing with religious regimens, they will be back into the world at the blink of an eye.

Luke 8:16 is also a warning to every believer to be careful that the light in you does not become darkness. Be careful not to cover up the light of Christ by your actions or attitudes. That would keep unbelievers from seeing the light and entering in. Second Corinthians 4:3–4 warns us of that very thing: "But even if our gospel is veiled, it is veiled to those who are perishing, whose minds the god of this age has blinded, who do not believe, lest the light of the gospel of the glory of Christ, who is the image of God, should shine on them." But I want to suggest to you that there is another way that darkness can be present.

The first thing a person does when he gets too much light is to cover or shut his eyes. Overbearing spiritual light that is forced upon a person emerging from the darkness of deception and sin will also cause the new believer to cover or shut his eyes. What is the difference between being in a dark room with no light and being in a lighted room with your eyes closed? There is no difference. In both cases, the person is blind and cannot see a thing.

In Acts 22, the apostle Paul talks about the moment when he met God on the road to Damascus. As he journeyed along the road, "a great light from heaven shone around me" (v. 6). Paul says this: "And since I could not see for the glory of that light, being led by the hand of those who were with me, I came into Damascus" (v. 11). Paul was blinded by the glorious light of God. It was brighter than he could stand—and it was several days before his sight was restored to him.

New believers may not be able to receive the fullness of God's light in the midst of their darkness immediately. Salvation is a process, and God continually takes us from one glory to the next. God will "turn up the light" in each person's life as that person's spiritual eyes are able to receive that light. When you allow God to "give the increase" (as the Word promises in 1 Corinthians 3:7), people do not retreat back into the world because the light was too bright for them to handle at that time.

Our instruction, as ministers of the gospel, is to feed the sheep. God provides the menu, and we serve it, but God is the one who makes the person grow!

Deprivation of Food

POWs are deprived of the food they need to nourish and keep their bodies healthy. Just so, we need to sure that we are not depriving a new believer of the spiritual food he or she needs to grow in Jesus. Eating is a natural principle that does not seem difficult to understand—if a person does not eat they will die. Not only do we need food, but we need well-balanced meals eaten on a consistent basis. If I ate lunch two days ago, no matter how nourishing it was, it is not going to do me any good at this moment. The growling in my belly is a sign that I have not eaten what I needed to sustain my body today.

It is God's Word that sustains our spiritual life. In 2 Timothy we read:

> All Scripture is given by inspiration of God, and is profitable for doctrine, for reproof, for correction, for instruction in righteousness, that the man of God may be complete, thoroughly equipped for every good work.
> —2 Timothy 3:16–17

It amazes me that people can believe that they can walk in God without being fed daily by the Word. I feel that it is safe to say that we can look at the spiritual signs in a person's life and be able to determine if there is a spiritual deficit of the Word in their life.

When a deficit can be detected, that person could be suffering from one of the following factors:

1. They are not being fed at all.
2. They are not being fed as often as they need to be fed.
3. They are not being fed enough.
4. They are eating the wrong kind of food.

A balanced spiritual diet is very important to the new convert. That person is a brand-new spiritual baby. They have been born again. Studies have shown that breast-fed babies are the healthiest of babies. The mother's milk has all the nutrients required for that child in her natural system.

I believe there is a spiritual correlation to a new convert. Although we must disciple and mentor new converts, there is nothing more important for that new convert than developing a close personal relationship with Father God in the baby stages of salvation. This time with God is more precious than the rarest jewel. During those personal moments God is able to pour His sustenance and nurture directly into the spiritual mouth of that newborn convert. That person receives the "milk" of the Word directly from God Himself.

God has done that in my own life. I walked out of the darkness of drug addiction, immorality, violence and failed relationships into God's marvelous light. You can read my testimony in my recently released books *Against All Odds* and *From a Mess to a Miracle*.[1] One of my greatest struggles after coming into the light of Jesus Christ was to hold on to the genuineness of my faith.

The key to my growth was the fact that God allowed me to be a spiritually breast-fed baby. I was raised up in the Lord overseas where I did not have contact with a lot of saints. As I look back, I treasure those moments with the Lord. He nourished me Himself as I spent time developing my personal relationship with Him.

So often the traditional "church system" seems strategically designed to kill our "first love." (See Revelation 2:1–7.) For example, I reached a time when it was no longer enough for me to get secondhand messages from God all the time. I wanted to hear from God for myself. I will never forget the first time I heard God's voice. I am thankful for the words that God has given people to speak into my life. There is a place for that. *But it is secondary to hearing "my Daddy" speak directly to me.*

Nothing can replace our personal time with the Lord! Our personal time with God sets the foundation to receive the Word from the one who feeds us. Many have a hard time receiving the Word in church because they have not spent time with God behind closed doors.

The first words I heard from God will be eternal in my heart. He said, "Seek the face of the Father!" At the time I had been asking God to speak to me, just as everybody else was saying that He was speaking to them. I had never heard God's voice. I had only been saved for a few months. I had begun a Bible study at a military installation in Frankfurt, Germany. I called myself a *gatherer.* I gathered the people and invited others to preach.

Every speaker told me that God wanted me to begin speaking. It was very frustrating because I did not even know where the books of the Bible were positioned. But in the middle of the night, God spoke to my heart with these words: "Seek the face of the Father!" That was all I needed; I began preaching the gospel the next day. The title of my first message was "Seek the Face of the Father."

It is not as important to hear from God as it is to respond properly to what God has said. When Jesus calls, you had better answer (and don't be slow about it)! Whether you are a breast-fed spiritual baby who is personally nourished by *El Shaddai,* the "breasted God," or you draw your spiritual milk from a bottle prepared by the pastor, you have a responsibility to eat. The more you eat in the Spirit, the more you will reap in the Spirit.

The enemy wants us to suffer from spiritual malnutrition. If he can get us to avoid receiving our spiritual milk, he knows there will be room for him to have a place in our lives. But when you eat a balanced meal in God, you close the doors to the enemy.

LEARNING HOW TO PRAY

Communication with God is a two-way street. It is important to be nourished and fed by God, but you must also learn how to communicate with Him through your prayers. The Bible says, "The effective, fervent prayer of a righteous man avails much" (James 5:16). To walk effectively in the light of Christ, you have to stay away from spiritual danger zones. You learn to do that as you learn the ways that you should pray. You must also learn the ways you *should not pray*. Let's take a closer look at the "Don'ts of Intercession." Each of the following types of prayer should be avoided.

Anxious prayer

When you pray, be watchful so that your flesh will not cause you to run ahead of God. Paul warned that there are things that can disqualify us concerning the gospel and cause us to become castaways (1 Cor. 9:27). In the sport of track and field, the number one way to get disqualified from a race is to jump out of the starting block too fast. It does not matter if you are the better runner; if you jump ahead, you have to pick up your block and watch the race from the sidelines.

God's Word teaches us over and over again to wait on God. Psalm 130 gives us the picture of waiting for God as a watchman waits for the end of a long night on watch:

> I wait for the LORD, my soul waits,
> And in His word I do hope.
> My soul waits for the LORD
> More than those who watch for the morning—
> Yes, more than those who watch for the morning.
> —PSALM 130:5–6

If you wait for the Lord, you shall not be put to shame (Isa. 49:23). The New Testament tells you to be anxious for nothing

(Matt. 6:34). Your life is in God's hands, and He alone knows when you should be ending one season of your life and moving on to the next. (See Ecclesiastes 3:1.)

Tainted prayer

Tainted prayers are prayers that are a mixture of your own will and God's will. Or they may be a mixture of sincere prayer tainted with the wrong motives. Whatever the case, God wants you to pray pure prayers.

Peter advises the believer that "the genuineness of your faith" will bring "praise, honor, and glory" to Jesus Christ (1 Pet. 1:7). God hates mixtures of godliness with worldliness. He would rather you be one way or the other. God chastened the church at Laodicea by telling them, "I know your works, that you are neither cold nor hot. I could wish you were cold or hot. So then, because you are lukewarm, and neither cold nor hot, I will vomit you out of My mouth" (Rev. 3:15–16).

This church hung out in the gray areas. God is advising us that it would be better for us to be either black or white (hot or cold) than to be lukewarm. That goes for our prayer life also. He wants us to make our specific requests known to him (Phil. 4:6).

Praying with our natural minds is also a form of tainted prayer. Romans 8:7 says that the carnal mind is at enmity against God. Praying with our natural minds will always come up against the true will and purpose of Christ. There is a way that seems right to the carnal mind, but the end of it is death (Prov. 14:12). There is life and death in the power of the tongue. When you pray the will of God, you speak life! When you pray in the spirit, you pray the perfect will of God. But when you pray with the understanding, you pray with wisdom.

Controlling prayer

Jesus instructed us to pray that the will of the Father be done in the earth realm. (See Luke 11:2–4.) This is why Jezebel hated true prophets—they spoke the will of God into the earth realm.

When the dogs ate the flesh of Jezebel, the only parts of that witch's body that were left were the palms of her hands, her feet and her skull. (See 2 Kings 9:35.)

These three body parts represent the characteristics of the spirit of Jezebel. The witch is dead, yet this spirit continues to come against the true Word of God being released in the earth today.

- *Hands*—represent an attempt to control the work of God
- *Skull*—represents mind control
- *Feet*—represent an attempt to lead our steps

Intercessors must come out of agreement with this spirit. You have to be careful when you are praying for things that have obsessed you. Obsession is a controlling spirit. Wherever there is a stronghold of control, the spirit of Jezebel is in the house. Praying in the spirit settles us in prayer.

There is a transition that takes place as you go into the presence of the Lord. Praying with a tormented mind will prompt wrong prayers. When Jesus began to pray in the Garden of Gethsemane on the night before His crucifixion, He referred to His need to transition into prayer by saying, "My soul is exceedingly sorrowful, even to death" (Mark 14:34). If Jesus experienced this…who are we to think that it will not affect us?

Jesus made a transition into the spirit and prayed, "Nevertheless, not what I will, but what You will" (v. 36). When Jesus said "nevertheless," He was saying, "Not what My mind is telling Me to do, but what the Spirit of God is telling Me to do." Renounce controlling prayers that get you caught up in your emotions, causing you to say the wrong things out of your mouth.

Trespassing prayer

Trespassing prayer is representative of eating from the tree of the knowledge of good and evil. When Adam and Eve ate of the forbidden tree, they began to know what God had not called them to know. Trespassing prayer is a type of psychic prayer, and it operates fluently through a "third eye." When Adam and Eve ate of the fruit, they opened a third eye. Intercessors must be careful not to go places in the spirit where God is not leading them to go.

Before their demonic experience, Adam and Eve walked with God in the cool of the day. When they partook of the fruit, their eyes were opened, and they knew they were naked. What made the difference after their rebellion? They were also naked before they ate the fruit. They had two eyes before they ate the fruit. But through their sin their spirits came together with their minds, and a third eye was opened. Rebellion is like the sin of witchcraft. Adam and Eve tapped into the occult.

There are lines in the spirit that have been drawn. In Hebrews 4:12 we read: "For the word of God is living and powerful, and sharper than any two-edged sword, *piercing even to the division of soul and spirit,* and of joints and marrow, and is a discerner of the thoughts and intents of the heart" (emphasis added). If you cross these spiritual boundaries, you begin to operate on the other side.

Religious prayer

In Matthew 6:5–8, Jesus warns us not to pray like religious folk. Some people get upset when I refer to the "religious spirit." Jesus called such people *hypocrites.* When people get upset about the truth, I know that I have done my job. Jesus hated religion because God hates religion—and that is why I hate religion. I do not have any hang-ups, and I am not going to burn down buildings to express myself, but I will take every chance that I get to stab that spirit with the truth! Jesus said, "Do not pray like them" (Matt. 6:5)!

Jesus broke religious spirits down into two categories.

- *Hypocrites*—the religious churchgoers who love to pray in public places so that they can be seen of men

- *Heathens*—the religious-acting pagans who use vain repetitions in their prayers

Jesus taught the disciples not to pray like these groups of people. He gave them a "prayer guideline," which is now known as *The Lord's Prayer*. The guidelines He gave us are principles by which believers should live. They are not food on which a Scripture-quoting demon should feed.

Isn't it perfectly understandable that the devil would pervert God's Word by taking God's own prayer, which was meant as a "training manual" for believers, and turn it into empty, meaningless, vain repetitions that heathens and religious groups pray.

Dead prayer

God is not moved to action by dead prayer. Heaven is ignited by prayer that is on fire. God desires for us to give Him our best. He is not interested in our leftovers. Anything less than our "firstfruits" is dead in God's eyes. (See Proverbs 3:9.) God expressed His displeasure with the Israelites for offering Him only their mediocre, leftover offerings:

> "You also say, 'Oh, what a weariness!' And you sneer at [the table of the LORD]," says the LORD of hosts. "And you bring the stolen, the lame, and the sick; thus you bring an offering! Should I accept this from your hand?" says the LORD.
> —MALACHI 1:13

God was not pleased with His people because they brought Him offerings that were lame and sick. Prayer is an offering unto God. God is insulted by lame, sick prayer. Just as God asked the Israelites this question, "Should I accept this lame offering?", so He lets us know that He will not accept our lame, dead prayers.

In this first chapter we have discovered the tactics the enemy will use to prevent us from moving through the process of the new birth to become the men and women of God that God wants us to be. We also took a look at some of the prayers God does not want us to pray as we develop a close, intimate relationship with Him. In the next chapter we will take a look at some of the ways we should pray.

Chapter 2

The Afterbirth

THE WORD OF the Lord says that the enemy comes to steal, kill and destroy (John 10:10). Immediately after a person has given his or her heart to God, satan creeps in to steal the seed of the Word. He wants to destroy everything that is of God. He even attempted to destroy Christ the Messiah when He was born. (See Revelation 12:1–6.)

Not only is the enemy a *seed eater,* but he is also a *fruit eater.* After you are born again, the fight begins! It is o-o-o-on in the spirit. We may as well 'fess up right now—we will have enemies as long as we are born again. Jesus had many enemies, but it was the way He dealt with His enemies that made Him stand out from among the rest.

Jesus dealt powerfully with His enemies, whether it involved physically kicking them out of the temple or submitting to the torment of the cross. The power in Jesus' ministry against His enemies came from the word that He spoke. When He faced the devil himself in the wilderness, Jesus' weapon was the Word of God.

In this chapter you will learn the principles of praying effectively. In chapter one you learned how useless it is to pray using wrong motives or methods. You saw that *religious* prayers—prayers that have become repetitious through familiarity—are totally ineffective against the enemy. God closes His ears to those kinds of prayer.

Be careful not to pray prayers just because you have heard others pray the same words. Our prayers need to be strategic and Spirit led. It will require strategic prayer to defeat our enemies. In the Book of Nehemiah we can see how Nehemiah prayed when he realized the enemy was attacking his men repeatedly as they rebuilt the walls of Jerusalem. He prayed:

> Hear, O our God; for we are despised: and turn their reproach upon their own head, and give them for a prey in the land of captivity: and cover not their iniquity, and let not their sin be blotted out from before thee; for they have provoked thee to anger before the builders.
>
> —NEHEMIAH 4:4–5, KJV

Nehemiah came against the evil work that had come against the work of God. He did not pray for them to be blessed! He prayed that the same thing that was sent against him would come upon their heads. In a sense, he reversed the curse.

These verses give two reasons that Nehemiah prayed the words he prayed:

1. The enemy was trying to stop the work of God.
2. They provoked God to anger before the builders.

Who were the *builders?* The Hebrew word for "builders" is *banah*, pronounced *baw-naw'*. It means "to begin to build, to set up, to obtain children." These definitions can apply to the apostolic and prophetic ministries in our world today. I believe that *the builders* represent the apostolic and prophetic foundation of the church. Ephesians 2:19–20 tells us that the household of God is "built" upon the foundation of the apostles and prophets, with Jesus being the chief cornerstone.

By attacking the builders, the devil was coming against the work of the church. He provoked God to anger with his attack, and we find God telling him: "Do not touch My anointed ones, and do My prophets no harm" (1 Chron. 16:22). When someone touches the work, that person touches the leader of the work. God does not want anyone touching the workers or the work of His church!

The *apostolic spirit* is a fathering spirit. It nurtures, protects and mentors. The apostolic ministry also gives births to souls. The apostolic ministry wins souls, but more than that, it gives birth to others who have vision to win more souls.

To discover more about the way you should pray in order to defeat your enemies, take a few minutes to read the scriptures and prayers included in Appendix A on page 186. These important principles will guide you as you develop a "ready-for-combat" prayer life.

CONFRONT THE BACKSLIDING SPIRIT

After you are born again, walking in the new birth is a wonderful experience. But don't forget that there are giants in the land. God has given you everything that you need to stand against the wiles of the enemy. Coming to Christ is the greatest decision that a person can ever make in life. The only thing greater, in my opinion, than coming to Christ is walking in the blessings of what He has promised us and *finishing the course.*

The enemy that attacks us in our walk in the new birth is a spirit I call the "backsliding spirit." In order to help you understand the strategies of this spirit so that you can recognize and avoid its snares, I want to talk about "afterbirth" in the natural.

Immediately after the birthing process is over and delivery of a baby has taken place, the first thing the doctor does is to get rid of the afterbirth. The afterbirth, or the placenta, has been the source of life for the baby while that baby was in the mother's womb. It was the source of everything the baby needed to sustain life until birth. It was the connection to life, and the baby was totally dependent upon the placenta for life itself.

Once the baby has left the birth canal, he or she is disconnected from that source. There is a clear comparison that you can make to your spiritual birth in Christ. You can compare the afterbirth in the natural birthing process to those things that attempt to follow you into the body of Christ. You must be totally disconnected from anything that would hinder your full delivery to Christ.

Deliverance is not just a condition; in 1 Peter 2:9 it is described as a transition in the spirit from a position of darkness into the marvelous light of Christ Jesus. Deliverance for the children of Israel entailed moving out of Egypt into the Promised Land. God always tells His people to move forward.

Anything from your past to which you return as a source is a type of *spiritual afterbirth*. It is poisonous and contaminated! The Word tells us that it would be better for us to have never known the way of righteousness than to turn back (2 Pet. 2:21). Verse 22 says that going back is like a dog returning to his vomit.

The word *vomit* is *exerama* in the Greek. It is related to another Greek word, *ex*. One of the meanings of *ex* is "to be remote or out of place in time or location." It is better to have never gotten to a certain place in God than to deviate from the faith. Hebrews 6:1–6 reads:

> Therefore let us go on and get past the elementary stage in the teachings and doctrine of Christ (the Messiah), *advancing steadily toward the completeness and perfection that belong to spiritual maturity.* Let us not again be laying the foundation of repentance and abandonment of dead works (dead formalism) and of faith [by which you turned] to God, with teachings about purifying, the laying on of hands, the resurrection from the dead, and eternal judgment and punishment. [These are all matters of which

you should have been fully aware long, long ago.]

If indeed God permits, we will [now] proceed [to advanced teaching]. For it is impossible [to restore and bring again to repentance] *those who have been once for all enlightened,* who have consciously tasted the heavenly gift and have become sharers of the Holy Spirit, and have felt how good the Word of God is and the mighty powers of the age and world to come. *If they then deviate from the faith and turn away from their allegiance—[it is impossible]* to bring them back to repentance, for (because, while, as long as) they nail upon the cross the Son of God afresh [as far as they are concerned] and are holding [Him] up to contempt and shame and public disgrace.

—AMP, EMPHASIS ADDED

These verses tell you that you can reach a place in your relationship with God where turning back will be something more serious than "something I am going through." There is a place of no return—a place of backsliding so serious that you can no longer be restored!

Because of a stiff neck and pride, you can go so far away from God that you can never experience His presence again. The ultimate separation from God is a trip to hell.

HELL IS A REAL PLACE

I am convinced that many do not really believe that hell exists. My walk with God is based on my love for Christ, and I need more than a divine revelation of hell to get saved. But it was the divine revelation of hell that pushed me toward a closer relationship with Christ. Now that I have the revelation and the relationship, the two bind together to strengthen me for the call of God on my life.

My ministry is, and always has been, controversial. Jesus' ministry was controversial. The reason the ministry of Jesus

Christ is controversial is because it proclaims the "Good News," or the gospel. Many do not understand the term *gospel*—although it is the Good News, it is not good news to everybody. Somebody is going to hell! But the good news is that we all have a choice!

Proclaiming the Good News will make some people mad. But as my favorite slang phrase asserts, *"Ain't nobody mad but the devil."* I must admit I enjoy casting out devils! I am comfortable doing what I am called to do. I operate in the deliverance ministry just as Creflo Dollar ministers fluently in the area of finances, Reinhard Bonnke operates with precision in evangelism and John Eckhardt is a father in the apostolic. All of these people are apostles in their vocations.

God told me that He would reveal to me the secrets of the strongman's camp and that I was to teach His people. To obey God I dare to go to places most people would avoid. Somebody has to do it, and I believe that it might as well be me. So I have no problem releasing mysteries from the dark side that God has revealed to me. It is a part of the gospel.

There are wonderful teachings on faith, financial stewardship, marriage and many more subjects about victorious living in Jesus. But they are not the whole story. It will do a person no good to know only one side of the story. Yes, the wealth of the wicked is stored up for the just, but you are going to have to go through hell to get it. The devil and his crew are not going to sit back and allow you to dance in and out of his camp with the goods.

The "gates of hell" is not just a place under the ground that is an entrance for bad people. The word *gates* is *pule* in the Greek. It means a doorway or portal or way of travel through which demons move from the underground to the earth realm. These portals are called *vortexes*. Witches and warlocks from around the world travel to certain locations where they know high demonic activity exists in order to worship these gateways. The "gates of hell" are spiritual assignments designed to hinder the will of God in the earth realm. They are forces assigned to keep the kingdom of God from coming in the earth realm.

In Matthew 16:18–19, Jesus encourages us that "the gates of hell" will not prevail against the church. He gives us keys to the kingdom. The word *keys* in this passage is *kleis* in the Greek. *Kleis* means "to shut down, lock up, close." This word has nothing to do with releasing or allowing. We have often used this warfare term in a way that is not scripturally correct. In this passage, the keys that Jesus gave us do not open or close. They only lock up and forbid to operate.

When we consider that Jesus was referring to the gates of hell, this meaning makes a lot of sense. He was not suggesting that we *release* or *allow* anything. Why would He want us to open or release anything in this sense?

However, the key of the house of David referenced in Isaiah 22:22 is a key that opens and closes. This word *key* in Hebrew is *maphteach* and means "key, opener."

A War Between Two Kingdoms

The source of the spirit of backsliding is the pit of hell. The devil has no worries about the people already in hell. But the gates of hell target new candidates. The enemy wants to increase the vision of the demonic kingdom.

Demons are released through the vortexes of the earth daily as they ignorantly attempt to stop the kingdom from coming. The devil is mentally retarded, and his thinking sometimes takes a while to catch up with him. He truly does not have the revelation that the kingdom has already come! In reality, the kingdom of God is only present to those who can receive the truth of what the kingdom is all about. Therefore, in his ignorance, the devil tries to bring hell on earth, not understanding that God is releasing His kingdom to come. Let's take a look at some things that manifest that the kingdom of God has come:

- The kingdom comes when the will of God is done—Matthew 6:10.
- The kingdom comes if you cast out demons by the Spirit of God—Matthew 12:28.
- The kingdom comes when the children are allowed to come to Jesus—Matthew 19:14.
- The kingdom comes when the last becomes first and the first becomes last (when the smallest seed sown becomes the greatest)—Mark 4:31–32.
- The kingdom comes when the sick are healed—Luke 10:9.
- The kingdom comes when men reject you for the gospel's sake, and you have to shake the dust from yourself—Luke 10:10–11.
- The kingdom comes when men do not walk by observation but get a revelation—Luke 17:20.
- The kingdom comes when the accuser of the brethren is cast down—Revelation 12:10.

There are some spiritual principles that have become the main targets of the gates of hell against the believer. These include:

1. The will of God for our lives
2. The ministry that God has given every believer to cast out devils (deliverance)—Mark 16:17
3. Ministry to the next generation; the devil wants to kill off our spiritual posterity
4. Changed lives, whereby Jesus delivers from the "guttermost to the uttermost"
5. The healing virtue of Christ in the earth realm
6. The privilege of suffering with Christ
7. The revelation that has been reserved for God's apostles and prophets today
8. The ability of the believer not only to cast out the devil, but also to bring down his kingdom (warfare)

The writer to the Hebrews warns us to "get past the elementary teachings of things like laying the foundation for repentance and dead formalism and of the faith by which you turn to God." (See Hebrews 6:1.) God is not saying that these things are unimportant. But He is saying that you do not need to keep learning the same things over and over again.

You can reach a level of maturity so that when you read the same scriptures, you get fresh revelation each time. I believe in discipleship and mentoring, but I see too many cases where as leaders we keep people on the milk too long. Babies do not make good soldiers. Hebrews tells us that some people have learned the same thing over to the point that they should be teaching it by now (Heb. 5:12). If God permits, you need to proceed to advanced teaching.

You should never neglect the simplicity of the gospel that you understood to receive Christ. Become mature in the principles of God in order to be a vessel used to manifest the coming of the kingdom in the earth realm. God did not tell us that He would pull down the strongholds and cast out devils for us. It is His pleasure to sit back and watch us do it. The devil is no match for the Lord of lords and King of kings! We are His tools.

Ezekiel said that when the bones in the valley stood up and came together, they became one stick in the hand of the Lord (Ezek. 37:17). Many argue that we are no match for the devil and that we should leave the devil to the Lord. But such thinking is contrary to the spiritual fact that Jesus gave us the keys—and He sat down. He gave us power and authority over all the power of the devil. You have that authority because God wants you to use it.

The Lord takes pleasure in seeing His children beat up on His enemy. You were born into a war! When you accepted Christ, you enlisted in God's army. After the new birth, it is not time to struggle with the afterbirth of what is trying to follow us into the kingdom. The devil is a trespasser and a violator. He will intrude on your rights because he does not obey the rules willingly. You have the authority to make him submit! Separate yourself from the afterbirth (of the new birth), and move toward your purpose in God.

God did not bring you out of Egypt to wander around in the wilderness for forty years, just as He did not intend for the Israelites to spend forty years wandering. The children of Israel could not cut the umbilical cord of their past. They insisted on keeping a connection "just in case."

God is removing all of your options. He will not allow you to go into the promised land with a double-minded attitude. You must have "another spirit." To be this way you must be separated. Separation was what gave Joshua and Caleb a "well-able-to-do-it" attitude (Num. 13:30). It is hard to enter into the promised land with people, places and things hanging on to you and refusing to go in. Separate yourself in every aspect of the word.

Remember that there are giants in the land. The new birth is all about separating yourself from the afterbirth and manifesting God's glory in the earth realm. To do this, you will have to cut down a few giants in life. Don't be scared! God has given you power over giants, but you must know how to deal with the strongman. You will learn how to do that in the next chapter.

Chapter 3

Who Is the Strongman?

B Y THE TIME you have completed this chapter, you will be able to *define what a strongman is, understand how he operates* and *identify different types* of biblical strongmen.

It is important to distinguish the difference between the *strongman* and an *evil spirit*. Both are evil spirits. But the strongman holds more rank and authority than a regular evil spirit. The strongman is the gatekeeper of the stronghold. He garrisons the stronghold, stationing troops to guard it, and secures its position.

In dealing with the strongman, you have to remember that he is guarding something valuable. Satan does not assign strongmen to strategic places that are not of value to him. If it is of value to satan, it has to be of some kind of value to you. The devil studies what is valuable to you, trying either to lock you in with it so that you cannot get out, or trying to lock you out so that you can never receive or achieve it.

SPOILING HIS GOODS

The strongman controls the traffic of the stronghold. One of your goals, when confronted with a strongman, must be to destroy the strongman's belongings, taking back from him those things he took from you. But how do you do that?

We often sing a chorus about going to the enemy's camp to take back what the enemy has stolen from us. How can you be sure that you can take it back? In Matthew 12:29, Jesus addressed that very issue by asking a very important question: "How can one enter a strong man's house and plunder his goods, unless he first binds the strong man?" You need an understanding about two things—the strongman's house and the strongman himself. Let's look first at the strongman's house.

The strongman's house

The strongman's house is the stronghold. This is the place where he stores all the things that he has stolen from you. Jesus tells us that before you can enter his house and take back anything, you must "first bind the strong man." The word *first* is *proton* in the Greek. It means "first in order of importance." Jesus is telling you to put first things first. In essence, He is saying, "Don't go running up into the enemy's camp without a game plan, because he has something waiting for you!"

What happens to a person who enters the strongman's camp to take back what was stolen from him without a plan that he follows carefully? That man becomes a prisoner of the camp! The strongman will let you into his camp with no struggle as long as you have no power over him. As long as you let him continue to run things, he'll let you in whenever. He knows that rather than you controlling him, he will be able to control you.

The devil likes it when you are a prisoner in the house of the strongman. As long as you are a prisoner, you are no threat to him. You will not be able to attack him from the outside. You can have the devil's goods without spoiling the devil's goods.

The wealth of the wicked is stored up for the just (Prov. 13:22). It is your responsibility to spoil the goods of the strongman. When you do not spoil the goods, you partake of the accursed thing. In order for the wealth to be transferred and blessed by God, the goods must be spoiled. The word *spoil* is *diarpazo* in the Greek. This word means "to plunder or seize." One of the meanings of the root word, *dia,* means "to avoid." Spoiling the goods of the strongman means taking his stuff and avoiding the spirits that come with the stuff.

If you cannot avoid the spirits that come with the stuff, you have partaken of the accursed thing and become a prisoner of the stronghold. As prosperous as a person may seem, that person can still be a prisoner of the stronghold.

I have learned that if you bind the strongman, you do receive the goods! But unless you stay in place to rule over the goods that you have taken back, those goods will rule over you. As we read in Mark 8:36, "For what will it profit a man if he gains the whole world, and loses his own soul?"

NAMING THE STRONGMAN

People often say that it is not important to know the specific names of spirits. I believe it is important, and I can provide testimonials to back up my belief. One example would be the experience of Monica, a young lady I have known for several years.

At one time, Monica had continual struggles with character issues like gossiping, integrity, jealousy and unforgiveness. Although she had been trained as an armorbearer, when she attended the services in churches where I was ministering, she often manifested more than the people in those churches. She had strong manifestations like falling on the floor and crawling around like a snake.

You should not be afraid of such manifestations, and you should not judge the person who has them. God's anointing will destroy the yoke of demonic control, but sometimes in order to destroy it, God has to bust it out. Because of the anointing on my life, at times spirits manifest around me, but those same spirits may never show up in a normal service. Although Monica had been attending church for several years, she never experienced a manifestation until she began walking in close relationship to me.

This is a biblically sound occurrence. People in the temple were going about their everyday business until Jesus came on the scene. When Jesus showed up, the demons cried out. Just because demons are not manifesting and crying out does not mean that they are not present. The anointing not only destroys the yoke, but it shines light on darkness and makes that which is hidden come out and be seen for what it really is.

The word *occult* is defined as "that which is hidden with the intention of never being seen." This is why we have so much witchcraft in the church. The enemy has crept in unawares. The Word of God tells us that "...the Lord comes, who will both bring to light the hidden things of darkness and reveal the counsels of the hearts" (1 Cor. 4:5).

When this happened, we immediately began intensive counseling and ministry to her. Despite this, we had the most difficult time getting the strongman out of this girl's life. A demon talked fluently through her. I hated this demon! It would try to embarrass her all the time. Finally the evil spirits in her made the mistake of giving us the name of the strongman. It was *Rajah*.

I looked that name up in dictionaries, encyclopedias and many kinds of Bible reference books, but I could not locate the name. Finally I found the name in an old occult dictionary from the library. *Rajah* was the name of an ancient occult spirit. Soon after that I discovered that several members of Monica's family had been witches who called on this god.

After some specific deliverance ministry from us, including identifying this spirit by name, she was totally set free! She has had several years of subsequent counseling from our ministry, but today she is walking with Jesus and living victoriously—outside the clutches of Rajah.

Since our experience with Monica, we have run into this spirit several times. Each time we quickly cut off his head and destroy his control.

The word *man* in *strongman* is *anthropos*. This word is related to the English word *anthropology*, which is the study of man. *Anthropos* means "an individual or certain man." It comes from another Greek word, *optomahee*, which means "to witness the personality, appearance or character of."

Demons take on personalities. They mimic the qualities, traits, character or behavior of people. In schizophrenic cases, a person may have many personalities. In actuality, they are being controlled by many demons that are acting out the traits of personalities they have picked up from people.

Before you can bind the strongman, you must witness the personality or character of the spirit. The name of the strongman has a lot to do with his character. By knowing his character, you can easily determine how he operates. Because I have a bachelor's degree in criminology from Florida State University, I am aware of the fact that detectives can learn a lot about a suspect by studying that person's character.

One time I was ministering to a group of Yoruba witches. The first young lady to approach me said that God had told her that I could help her to be released from the ruling spirits that governed over her head. She was studying to be a white witch, and she told me that I had to know the names of the ruling spirits. She taught me the names of the gods she prayed to. They are called *orishas* in a voodoo religion. There are many orishas, but I became familiar with a few: *Ogun, Oshun* (these two are road gods, "crossroads"), *Obatala* and *Shango*. I often see these gods exalted on television shows and honored in exhibits in museums. When I prayed for her, the demons were so strong in her life that she levitated off the floor. But she was delivered through the power of Jesus Christ and is still delivered today.

The word *strong* in *strongman* is *ischuros* in the Greek. This word refers to ability and strength. When Scripture makes reference to "a strongman spirit," it is pointing out a spirit that is a specialist. A strongman spirit has strong abilities and power in the area of demonic activity to which it has been assigned. One example is the strongman Leviathan, who is the king (or the specialist) over the children of pride. (See Isaiah 27:1.)

DEMONIC CHARACTERISTICS

Demonic entities are classified by their characteristics and abilities. In the eighth chapter of Luke, Jesus encountered and healed a demoniac man. Jesus asked the demon, "What is your name?" The demon told Jesus, "My name is Legion; for we are many" (Mark 5:9). The man's response told Jesus several things:

- Legion was the chief ruling spirit in the person's life.
- There were many spirits that accompanied him.
- The use of the terms "my" and "we" indicated the significance of the roles of the demons.

"My" represented the strongman, and "we" represented the other spirits. Jesus describes a demon that leaves a man but promptly asserts, "I will return to *my* house from which I came" (Matt. 12:44, emphasis added). This demon was the strongman, and Jesus said that upon his return he would be accompanied by seven other spirits more wicked than himself. The strongman is not necessarily the more wicked spirit in a person's life. He is the gatekeeper. His importance is his position. He has power to control the demonic traffic in an area of a person's life.

THE IMPORTANCE OF NAMES

In Mark 5:9, the word *name* is *onoma* in the Greek. According to the meaning of this word, Jesus asked the demon:

- What are you called?

- What is your authority?
- What is your character?

The word *onoma* means, "What are you called in the spirit? What is your character? By what authority do you operate?" This is how we destroy devils at Spoken Word. We identify them by name.

Names are extremely important to demons. If a demon does not recognize the name of the person attempting to destroy it, that person has no authority over that demon. When the seven sons of Sceva tried to get a man delivered from demonic control, the demons embarrassed them by refusing to leave and retorting, "Jesus I know, and Paul I know; *but who are you?*" (Acts 19:15, emphasis added).

There are biblical names that carry a stigma because of the fact that evil spirits used these people in terrible ways against God. These names include Cozbi, Balaam, Korah and Cain, and they will be remembered forever because of their evil acts.

What you do "for" or "against" God (without repentance) will be forever attached to your name. The following scriptures give a few examples:

> The memory of the righteous is blessed, but the name of the wicked will rot.
>
> —Proverbs 10:7

> A good name is to be chosen rather than great riches.
>
> —Proverbs 22:1

These scriptures help us to realize: "We are what our name is." You take on the character of whatever you allow to place a covering over you or to have authority over you. If Christ is my covering, I will display His characteristics in my own life. But if satan is my covering, I will display his demonic characteristics. Every time a person calls me *Kim Daniels*, that person is reinforcing the character of what I really am in the spirit. May I always display the character of my Father God!

The strongmen that work for satan take on the characteristics of their father. The devil has always desired to exalt himself above God. Lucifer said, "I will exalt my throne above the stars of God" (Isa. 14:13). The word *throne* is *kicce,* and it means "a false covering or to clad self." Satan and his demons still try to exalt themselves above God. Paul talks about the high thing that exalts "itself" against the knowledge of God in 2 Corinthians 10:5. The word *itself* is *autos* in the Greek, and it refers to the exaltation of an individual.

GATEKEEPERS

Individuals who have clad themselves with a false covering are not true gatekeepers. The Pharisees pretended to be the "keepers of true religion," but Jesus recognized their pretense. When the Pharisees confronted Jesus, He told them, "You are of your father the devil" (John 8:44). False gatekeepers are individuals who have clad themselves with a false covering. In other words, they have inherited a bad name in the spirit.

The Bible identifies godly gatekeepers, recognizing them by name. But it also identifies false gatekeepers. Gatekeepers are biblical types of a strongman. They control the traffic that flows through the doorways. There are many other gatekeepers in the Bible, but the chart on the next page will give you an idea of the two kinds of gatekeepers and what the function is for each.

Let's take a closer look at these gatekeepers.

GODLY GATEKEEPERS

- **Daniel (Authority)**—He sat at the gate of the king of Babylon (Dan. 6:2).

- **Mordecai (Intercession)**—He sat at the king's gate without compromise when his life was in danger (Esther 5:9).

- **Man at the Gate Beautiful (Deliverance)**—He sat at the gate of the temple and was not ashamed of his deliverance (Acts 3:1–10).

DEMONIC GATEKEEPERS

- **Lot (Compromise)**—He sat at the gate of Sodom (Gen. 19:1).

- **Tamar (Deception)**—She sat at the gate of the city (Gen. 38:14).

- **Bigthan and Teresh (Mutiny)**—They sat at the king's gate desiring to lay hands on him (Esther 2:21).

- **The women weeping for Tammuz (Idolatry)**—These women wept for Tammuz (baby Nimrod) in the gate of the Lord's house (Ezek. 8:14).

DEMONIC STRONGMEN LISTING

I want to give you an introduction to some of the specific demons described in God's Word. Each of these has specific characteristics and a specific assignment against God.

Incubus—Genesis 6:2

Incubus is a demon said to cause nightmares. It is an evil

spirit or demon that, in medieval times, was thought to descend upon women and have sexual intercourse with them.

Succubus—Genesis 6:2

Succubus is an evil spirit or demon thought, in medieval times, to descend upon sleeping men and have sexual intercourse with them. Some victims of this spirit have testified that these spirits can sometimes have both sex organs. These demons open the door to sexual perversions such as masturbation and homosexuality. These demons respond to human desire and will cause body parts to do the things they would do in natural sexual acts. These doors may also be opened to a person if that person associates with someone in his or her house who is entertaining sex demons.

Be careful whom you allow to hang around, come into or sleep at your house.

Lilith—Isaiah 34:14

Lilith means "night." She is a female demon that lives in desolate places. Lilith is called the "night hag." *Lamashtu* is the Babylonian counterpart. Isaiah refers to her (although there is no male or female in the spirit) as the demon of the desert (Isa. 34:14). In 1975 Lilith was adopted by the American Jewish feminist movement and is regarded as a symbol of strength and independence to women. She is the underlying root demon when it comes to the women's feminist movement. She is the avowed enemy of newborn babies. She vows to kill newborn babies before they reach the age of one year.

To protect a newborn from this evil spirit, anoint the bassinet and bind the spirit of Lilith. Molech is the source or root demon of abortions and works closely with the spirit of Lilith. These two spirits are at enmity with the woman and her seed. Lilith is assigned to kill the ability to reproduce. This demon would rather get a child before it's born. If barrenness, abortion or miscarriage is unsuccessful, then crib death is the ultimate goal.

Python—Acts 16:16

Python is the Greek name, and *Putho* is the name of the region where the famous Delphi oracles were located. The word *divination* means "python" in the Greek. The spirit of python is the spirit in opposition to the adder spirit. An adder is a small poisonous, venomous snake. The python is a large, nonpoisonous snake. The adder would poison, but the python, because he has no poison or venom in him, would slowly squeeze his enemy to death. The spirit of python or divination slowly squeezes the life out of a person.

A woman who was "possessed with a spirit of divination" followed Paul and Silas for a while as they traveled in Europe (Acts 16:16–17). After tolerating her for a few days, the man of God turned around and dealt with the spirit. The spirit of *python* and the *divination* spirit are closely associated with the spirit of *mammon*. The spirit of *mammon* relates to riches (not necessarily money—but anything that is material and of value) of this world.

People operate in the supernatural for money and power. The enemy knows this need for money and power and will use this human need, coming to you in a pretty package.

Religion—2 Timothy 2:15–18

I realize that there is a pure religion, but my goal is to expose the counterfeit. The religious spirit walks closely with the spirit of python. It sucks the Jesus out of its victims. The religious spirit infiltrates and sets the atmosphere through a strong belief system and traditional paradigms. The religious spirit is the strongman of strongmen. It stands in the door of the church and allows other spirits like perversion, leviathan, greed, molestation and control to enter. These spirits hide behind the cloak of the religious spirit.

The religious spirit is a type of *Baal of Peor* (Num. 25:3). Baal of Peor is the "lord of the opening." The Bible refers to the "iniquity of Peor" and the "matter of Peor" (Josh. 22:17; Num. 25:18). The people of God turned their hearts to idols and worshiped the spirit of Peor. God does not take kindly to His people mess-ing around with other gods.

The significance of this spirit is that it brings a curse on the entire congregation. In Joshua 22:16–20, Joshua reminded the congregation of the iniquity of Peor and how they were still affected by that curse. He reminded them of Achan's sin of par-taking of the accursed thing, pointing out to them how the entire congregation suffered. Their idolatry of Baal Peor is the reason that many of the children of Israel were left to die in the wilderness and denied entrance to the Promised Land.

Idolatry is designed to keep us out of the promised land. When idolatry links up with the religious spirit, it forms a demonic alliance that causes God's people to walk in a sublimi-nal bondage, which is hard to reach with deliverance. Baal Peor is the spirit that spearheads the traditional paradigms to which so many people cling. The Word of God warns us to "study to shew thyself approved unto God, a workman that needeth not to be ashamed, rightly dividing the word of truth" (2 Tim. 2:15, KJV). It also tells us that profane and vain babblings will turn into more ungodliness (2 Tim. 2:16). The spirits of error and pride set up paradigms to lead congregations of people into things that are futile to God.

Haman—Esther 3:1

Haman comes into the body of Christ and grows up with the church. The wheat and tares grow up together. The spirit of Haman represents the tares that grow up in the church. They have been around for so long that now they have positions over God's people. The spirit of Haman is in the pulpit, in the choirs and is walking in a false apostleship. Haman gets in the body of Christ as a familiar spirit. He targets decision-making positions to secure his ability to kill God's people. This is a strong religious spirit.

In dealing with the spirit of Haman the curse must be reversed. Haman comes to curse, to kill and destroy. There is only one way to deal with the spirit of Haman. He will not submit because he is on assignment. He is sent for only one reason, to kill God's people. This spirit uses gifted (charismatic) people. They usually have the ability to draw crowds. A spiritual alliance that operates fluently with Haman is "Hymenaeus" (the king of religion or "what I believe is right"). (See 2 Timothy 2:17–18.)

Necromancy—Deuteronomy 18:11

Necromancy is the act of communicating or coming into contact with the dead. There is no reason for needing to come into contact with or to communicate with the dead.

Nehushtan—2 Kings 18:4

Nehushtan refers to the brazen serpent that Moses made when God healed the people of poisonous vipers. (See Numbers 21:4–9.) It represented idolatry and spiritual dependency on things outside of God's power. *Nehushtan* means "brazen trifle, disrespectful, rude, in self-confidence, having no value, a waste." God had a one-time purpose for Nehushtan, but with idolatrous hearts the people continued to look to the snake on the pole for healing. People kept their eyes on Nehushtan and took their eyes off God.

The Bible said that the sons of the priest offered strange fire unto the Lord (Num. 3:4). Any man-made sacrifice is strange fire to God and just another Nehushtan. God will use things for a time or season. But people often get so caught up in the moment that they are not prepared to move on with the glory cloud. This often occurs with revival meetings that go past the sanctioning of God.

Today the national medical symbol is still a pole with a snake wrapped around it. People are still looking to man-made buildings above God for their healing. Hospitals and doctors are a blessing, but Jesus is *the blessing!*

Behemoth—Job 40:15

This spirit walks hand in hand with the king of pride, Leviathan. Behemoth is a spirit that generally operates in men (but this is not always the case). He's very strong, well built, and his strength is in his loin area. His bones are like iron bones, and his backbone is as strong as a cedar. Behemoth is very greedy and gluttonous. He can never get enough! He will suck up an ocean with his mouth thinking that he is big enough to hold it. He bites off more than his stomach can handle. He anticipates more than he can take.

He is the demon that hides behind male supremacy. The Muslim culture with its mentality about women is rooted in the spirit of Behemoth. Behemoth is deceptive. This spirit makes it impossible for a man to be satisfied with one woman. I believe that Behemoth was the spirit that was on King Solomon. He thought he had many wives, but in actuality... *they had him!* His wives turned his heart away from God. Every woman Solomon slept with gained access to his spirit within. The result was a schizophrenic, confused mind. He became unstable in all his ways.

Leviathan—Job 41

Leviathan is the king over the children of pride. Job 41:22 says, "Strength dwells in his neck." Pride and rebellion walk hand in hand. Rub your hand across the back of your neck. There is no flexibility in your neck. It is firm like a brick.

God called Leviathan a "stiff-necked" spirit. When dealing with Leviathan, you must also deal with all the demons that protect Leviathan (scales). The pride hides in the scales. Bind all the spirits that cover and garrison him, because Leviathan is the king of pride. These are alliances of legions that cover up the real problem to protect the strongman.

Because there is so much to discover about this spirit of Leviathan, I have written an entire chapter on the topic in my recently released book *From a Mess to a Miracle*.[1]

Poltergeist

In German, *polter* means "to make a sound or noise." *Geist* is the German word for ghost. So poltergeist is the spirit that gets in houses and buildings and makes noises. It is a mischievous spirit. Poltergeist is the root spirit of what is known as "haunted houses." This spirit gets in sound systems at the church and in computers in the bedroom. It causes doors to open and close without explanation.

This demon comes to release confusion and fear. It is also specially assigned against children. It targets children in order to open doors for other demons to communicate with them— through things like toys, dolls and stuffed animals. If you saw the movie *Poltergeist,* you were able to notice that the demon began with toys and by manifesting through the television. For some reason this spirit reveals itself to little children. Many call the demons "secret friends."

When a young man I once knew was eleven years old, he experienced a strange occurrence. One night when he was not feeling well, he was awakened by what he calls cute little bears that were running all over the blanket he had over him as he slept. He said that there were hundreds of these little creatures. They looked like stuffed animals, but they talked. He described them as being nice to him.

He was thirsty and got up to get a glass of water. He remembers inviting the bears to go to the kitchen with him. The bears never left the room, but when he returned, they were all gone. This was not a dream. From that time to now, that young man has had an uncontrollable obsession with stealing cars. He is locked up in a juvenile facility as I am writing. If it were not for the prayers and spiritual warfare of his family, he would be serving ten years to life for his previous violations. He is still very young, and his family is believing God for his deliverance.

I believe that when this young boy invited the spirits to go to the kitchen with him, they gained access to his spirit and entered his body. Since that time his entire personality has changed. It is important for parents to pay attention to the things that our children share with us and to bind "the things that go bump in the night"! I have ministered to hundreds of

children who have had these demonic experiences. Be aware—
there is a boogieman!

Rabshakeh—2 Kings 18:19

The *Rabshakeh* spirit is highly trained by satan (Sennacherib)
himself. His job is to release fear and discouragement against
our faith. This spirit makes a person question God as their
source. The Rabshakeh spirit tells you who you are not, what
you cannot do and what you cannot have. He also threatens you
about what he is going to do.

In 2 Kings 18, the Rabshakeh from Lachish states that he
comes to steal what you already know. He knew that Hezekiah
trusted in and leaned on the Lord, and he came to steal that trust
and confidence. (See 2 Kings 18:19–20.) This spirit comes to
those who already have confidence in the Lord so that he can
steal it. He is in direct opposition to spiritual leadership. It is his
character to speak to the hearts of the people to question their
leadership. If the Rabshekeh is speaking to you, you are on the
right track. Just don't let him steal your confidence in God.

Cockatrice—Isaiah 59:5

The word *cockatrice* means "she who treads." The cockatrice is
a legendary serpent that is supposedly hatched from a cock's egg
and has power to kill by a look. Though this creature is mytho-
logical in nature, there is a true spiritual connotation to its meaning and existence. The spirit of cockatrice is a mind-blinding
spirit, and it sets up its stronghold in the eyes of its victim.

Isaiah 14:29 clearly notes that "out of the serpent's root shall
come forth a cockatrice, and his fruit shall be a fiery flying serpent" (KJV). To defeat this spirit, you must curse the cockatrice
spirit to the root. If there is a root left, the result will be
demonic growth. Its power is in the nesting or dropping off
of demonic seeds. The danger is in the eggs of the cockatrice.

I have personally dealt with this spirit in key leaders in ministry. These leaders drop eggs into the heart of the people in the
congregation, causing them to leave the church. Even when a

leader who is troubled by this spirit leaves a ministry, that leader may have dropped the eggs of this spirit into the lives of many of the people left behind. Their lives are still affected by his rebellion because of these eggs. The cockatrice spirit and the spirit of pharaoh are closely related, because the cockatrice spirit is also related to the backsliding demon. A person backslides in his or her heart long before that person leaves the church. This spirit has a strong assignment against anointed spiritual leadership. I also have an in-depth teaching on this spirit in my book *From a Mess to a Miracle* in the chapter called "Snake Season."[2]

Pharaoh—Exodus 14:5–9

Pharaoh is the ultimate backsliding demon. Pharaoh will only allow you to go as far as the Red Sea in achieving your deliverance. Pharaoh is a type of devil. In Exodus 10:20 we see that the Lord hardened Pharaoh's heart to keep the people in bondage. The word *exodus* means "to exit or come out of or to be delivered." Matthew tells us that once a demon is cast out of a man, it comes back to reclaim its territory with seven times more power. Just as Jezebel was a natural woman who died a natural death, but the spirit that controlled her (the spirit of Jezebel) remained on earth after her death, so does the spirit of Pharaoh. This spirit is still running behind people who have been delivered to take them back to Egypt.

Pharmakeia—Galatians 5:20

Pharmakeia is the Greek word for *witchcraft* in Galatians 5:20. It means "medication by magic." This spirit is directly related to drug addition. The key work of this spirit is mood altering. Be watchful of any drug that has chemicals that alter your mood. These substances lead to dependency, and dependency leads to idolatry! Pharmakeia is the strongman of the stronghold of crack, heroin, alcoholism and prescription drugs.

STRONGMEN EVIDENT IN
WOMEN OF THE BIBLE

Athaliah—2 Kings 11:1

Athaliah was the stepdaughter of Jezebel. This spirit is not as overtly active as the spirit of Jezebel. It operates behind the scene. Athaliah hungers for total rule. This is a bloodthirsty spirit. Aware that its demise rests with the seed of its victims' heirs, it tries to kill off the heirs.

Bathsheba—2 Samuel 11:2

Bathsheba means "daughter of abundance." The power of this spirit is in her beauty—she has a look that will kill at one glance. (See Cockatrice.)

Cozbi—Numbers 25:18

Cozbi means "voluptuous" or "unrestrained pleasure." Numbers 25:18 speaks of "the matter of Cozbi," referring to a time when the hearts of the people were turned to idols. The Israelites were warned never to marry women who served other gods.

Delilah—Judges 16:18

Delilah means "temptress." This spirit is assigned directly against the anointed of God. She seduces leaders and leaves them with no power. She pretends to be interested in the deeper things of God, but her goal is to get her victims to lay their heads in her lap. She pursues her victims until total incapacitation has been achieved. She leaves her victims blind and powerless. She is in it for the money, and she has the ability to love and hate at the same time.

Eve—Genesis 1–4

Eve means "life" through rebellion. This spirit kills the spouse's relationship with God through ungodly influence. Someone manifesting this spirit may appear to be the perfect mate in the eyes of other people, but this spirit controls and manipulates the man behind the scenes. This spirit causes the woman to hang out with "spiritual snakes," which influence her. She does not let her husband know about her goings and comings until it is too late. She listens to "snake talk" all day long, and then comes home to transfer the spirit to her husband. Because the husband allows her to operate in this capacity, the home is dysfunctional, affecting the couple's ministry or church life as well.

Sapphira—Acts 5:1

Sapphira means "good." When this spirit influences a person, that person cannot discern the difference between a "good thing" and a "God thing." Sapphira is a strong religious spirit. Sapphira and her husband had a form of godliness, but denied the power thereof. They gave on the outside but hoarded in their hearts. They were religious hypocrites. This is a hoarding spirit that tries to be on the top in life. Her allegiance is to her husband and her career. She will go to hell, if she has to, to hold on to them. This is also a subliminal spirit of idolatry that comes from having wrong priorities in one's life.

Tamar—Genesis 38

The spirit of *Tamar* is overly ambitious. She will do whatever it takes to get what she wants. She has no loyalty to a man. She will sleep with his father and brothers. Tamar's one goal is to secure her future. She will marry for money, fame or position. She is a type of false gatekeeper. She sat at the gate of the city. This spirit operates in the spirit of black males and will keep a man by holding something over his head. She wears a veil in the spirit and cannot be easily detected. She is a harlot at heart.

Vashti—Esther 1

Vashti is the spirit that causes women to run from their calling. This spirit always makes excuses for not coming into the presence of the king. She has no prayer life. Vashti is too caught up with her personal problems to answer the call. Someone else always gets Vashti's position because she is never in place.

It should be noted that although these spirits are assigned most of the time to attack women, they are not limited to the female gender. For example, the spirit of Jezebel can operate through a man also.

In this chapter, we have taken a close look at many of the strongmen identified in the Bible. Not only are you now aware of their existence, but you can also identify many of the specific characteristics they have by which they try to manipulate and control the children of God. Let's read on to discover the tools and methods you have as a believer to defeat the strategies of these strongmen and destroy their influence upon your life.

Chapter 4

Dealing With the Spirit of Magnification

S INCE THE BEGINNING of time, the enemy has desired to be more than he was—more powerful, more recognized, more important. It rankles the devil to the core to know that *only El Shaddai* is "more than enough!"

Before his fall from glory, Lucifer had it going on in the spirit. He had an awesome position. His beauty goes down in the history books, and his fame can be compared to none. When the devil fell from glory, his desire to "be more" never left him.

> For you have said in your heart:
> "I will ascend into heaven,
> I will exalt my throne above the stars of God;
> I will also sit on the mount of the congregation
> On the farthest sides of the north;
> I will ascend above the heights of the clouds,
> I will be like the Most High."
>
> —Isaiah 14:13–14

The earth realm is satan's transition to his demise. He tried to lift himself up in heaven and was cast down to earth. He is en route to being the smallest creature ever created.

Yet you shall be brought down to Sheol,
To the lowest depths of the Pit.
Those who see you will gaze at you,
And consider you, saying:
"Is this the man who made the earth tremble,
Who shook kingdoms?"

—ISAIAH 14:15–16

The revelation of this passage is enough to take us to another level of authority in Christ Jesus! Let's review the path that Lucifer took. He held a high position in heaven. He was cast down to earth and is now on his way to eternal damnation. He was in heaven in the midst of an opportunity, but now he roams the earth in his vengeance.

Satan is also an evil magician and a master of trickery. Because he longs "for more," He often "transforms himself into an angel of light" in an attempt to deceive the believer (2 Cor. 11:14). He will use whatever means possible to ensnare a believer. He is a master delusionist. The Bible tells us that he is "seeking whom he may devour" (1 Pet. 5:8).

Yet God promises His people protection from the wiles and devices of the evil one. Weapons may form against the believer, but they will not prosper (Isa. 54:17). God's promise of protection is much greater than satan's delusion of destruction. But it is vitally important that you learn this truth: The supernatural manifestations that occur in your life are dependent upon your ability to discern each situation. The one that is greater in your eyes will manifest his glory in your life. If God is greater, it will be His glory that is manifested in your life. If satan is greater—then there is a satanic glory!

The proper word for satanic glory is *nimbus* or *halo*. It represents that which is considered sacred or holy. We often see pictures of Jesus with halos around His head. We also see halos pictured around the heads of angels. But I have found no biblical proof of angels with halos on their heads. This is a secular creation and has nothing to do with the truth. On the contrary, I have found proof that a nimbus is demonic and strongly related to witchcraft.

What is the significance of this false glory? This is the spirit that satan himself abides in. The devil has no real glory, so he has to create a glory for himself. Because he is not the creator, but only a created being, this task is very difficult for him to achieve. The only way he can get glory is through the spirit of deception, because all true glory belongs to the Lord Himself. The devil gets false glory by blinding the eyes of men.

The only way the devil can blind the eyes of men is by hiding the gospel from them. The Word of the Lord reads:

> But if our gospel be hid, it is hid to them that are lost: in whom the god of this world hath blinded the minds of them which believe not, lest the light of the glorious gospel of Christ, who is the image of God, should shine unto them.
> —2 Corinthians 4:3–4, kjv

The word *lost* in this scripture means "them that are perishing." Any person whose mind has been blinded by satan is perishing. Satan's only reason for blinding minds is to hide the truth of the gospel of Jesus Christ.

The avenue by which he blinds the minds of people is by manipulating them to walk the "road of unbelief." There are levels of unbelief. One level is the person who becomes an atheist or agnostic because of unbelief. But another level of unbelief that I believe is worse than that of either an atheist or agnostic is that of a *double-minded man!* James reveals that a "double-minded man" is "unstable in all his ways" (James 1:8). Such a man will receive nothing from God.

Double-minded means to be dubious or two-minded. It is the same as being lukewarm, or trying to have "a little bit of both" worlds. God said that He would prefer for us to be hot or cold.

Accepting Jesus is a choice that you make. You must remember that God is a God who draws lines.

- He used Moses to draw the line—"Who is on the Lord's side?" (Exod. 32:26, kjv).

- He used Elijah to draw the line—"How long will you falter between two opinions?" (1 Kings 18:21).

- He used Joshua to draw the line—"As for me and my house, we will serve the Lord" (Josh. 24:15).

We have a choice to make, not only in accepting Jesus as Lord and Savior, but also in taking Him at His Word. The gospel is not bound between the Books of Genesis and Revelation. There is no book that could contain all that truth! The full gospel includes every word that proceeds out of the mouth of God. When the Holy Spirit speaks a word to our heart concerning our personal affairs, it is always in accordance with the written Word of God.

MAGNIFICATION AND IMAGERY

A "Word-based word" from God is called a *rhema* word, which means "the spoken Word of God." This is the word "that takes feet" and goes forth to accomplish the will of God in your life. When God gives you a *rhema* word, you have to take Him at His word.

Let me give you an example. It is easy to believe that God parted the Red Sea because we read it in the Bible. On the other hand, when God tells us that He will part the Red Sea of cancer in our lives, it is hard to believe. I know that you love God and want to believe Him, but the real problem is that the things you are facing seem so "BIG"! This is the trick of the enemy. He operates through magnification and imagery. Let me define the two:

- **Magnification**—"To make something appear greater than what it really is." When Lucifer rebelled against God, he declared: "I will exalt my throne above the stars of God...above the heights of the clouds. I will be like the Most High" (Isa. 14:13–14). Since that time, he has roamed around "like a roaring lion" (1 Pet. 5:8). He comes in like a flood, trying to raise his status and to heighten and intensify his power at any cost. The spirit of magnification puts a magnifying glass on him.

- **Imagery**—"The production of mental images or sounds through erroneous perception arising from misrepresentation; closely related to hallucination, which is mental wandering." The foundation of curses sent by witchcraft against the born-again believer is imagery. Imagery is only real if we receive it to be so. Jesus really has all power, and satan has to operate with a counterfeit authority. The devil has been stripped of all power.

As a believer you must get a true revelation of the Greater One on the inside of you! The devil is spending his time in the earth realm deceiving as many as he can. He tricked Adam out of the dominion that God gave him, but Jesus came and hijacked hell and took dominion back. Not only was Lucifer cast down, but satan was beat down at the showdown in hell.

Jesus stripped satan of all authority. He took the keys of hell, death and the grave. Because Lucifer wanted to be *first*, Jesus made him *last*. The devil does not have a choice; it only looks as if he is having his way. Imagery and magnification are all that he has left. He has no true power. Jesus said, "I have ALL POWER!" That leaves none for the devil.

The only power the devil has is the power you give him in your mind. Satan has a big magnifying glass that he carries with him everywhere he goes. He still wants to "be like" God. Is there something the devil knows that most men do not know? The devil wanted to be like God, but God made us in His image. Can you imagine the devil's horror? The devil hates you because you look like he wants to look (like God). Not only did God make us to look like Him, but He also gave us rule over the devil. He gave us power over all the power of the enemy.

In the end, when everything is said and done, the Bible says that kings will look at satan and ask, "Is this the man...?" (Isa. 14:16). He will be revealed for all his *un*glorious deception! Though he craved glory, he will receive only disgrace. Isaiah 14:15 describes the best picture I can imagine about satan. Satan himself is pinned on the walls of hell. His magnifying glass has finally been removed, and the great men of this world are looking at him with shame and discussing amongst themselves, "Is this the man?"

I am sure that the realization of the truth will be horrible. Many people will suddenly realize that they have been following a loser—one who has no power at all. Graffiti about satan will be smeared on the walls of hell denouncing him as a loser and a deceiver.

As a believer, put the devil to open shame in your life now! I beg of you, do not wait until it is too late! Cast down the magnifying glass the devil has used to blow up the importance of the situations in your life. Cunningly he makes things seem so much bigger than what they really are. The sin of it all is that he makes you believe that *what you face* is bigger than *whom you serve!*

If God says that you are healed by His stripes, then you are healed—that is how it is. The devil gets a kick out of distracting us with things that are not real. Several years ago when I was five months pregnant with my twins, I was preaching at a Wednesday night service at our church. A lady whom we knew to be a practicing witch came into the meeting. This woman had told us of many *phantom pregnancies*—she was always claiming to be pregnant but never had any babies.

During these phantom pregnancies her body reacted as if she were pregnant. She even experienced an enlarged stomach. On this Wednesday evening, she attempted to speak to me, but I avoided her after the service. My husband and I went home, and the moment I stepped into the bathroom, blood began to gush from my body. We quickly wrapped towels around my body to stop the flow from getting on everything. I changed my clothes quickly, wrapped myself in new towels and got in the car for a trip to the emergency room.

On the way to the hospital, I called my intercessors. These words came out of my mouth: "I am on my way to the emergency room, and I appear to be having a miscarriage, *but it is not real!*" I was as surprised by the words that came out of my mouth as the intercessors were. I had no revelation of what was coming out of my mouth, but the Greater One was speaking from inside of me. God spoke through me that night, even though my natural mind could not understand what my body was going through.

I came in agreement with the Holy Ghost and continued to confess, "It is not real!" Though I made an effort to get the proper professionals to diagnose my predicament, I refused to believe the report the enemy was blowing up in my face. When I arrived at the emergency room, I was rushed into a crisis room as a woman experiencing a miscarriage. But I left the hospital a little while later with no signs of trouble.

The doctor's report stated that there were no signs of bleeding in my uterus. They gave me a clean bill of health. They suggested that I must have had a hard day and was just imagining the symptoms! I guess my husband had had a hard day also, and we were both tripping.

What the doctors did not realize is that they were right—it was an image, but it had been sent illegally. My husband and I sent the witchcraft back to the pit of hell where it came from. The witch at the service had cursed my womb. She did not comprehend that she could not curse one whom God had blessed.

Her curse could not attach itself to my body. As I returned home to find the bloody garments in the sink, I began to worship the Lord and thank Him for His awesome delivering power.

Get to the place where you can magnify God over the devil.

Yes, the devil is busy, and he does come in like a flood (I am a witness to that). But the overriding truth is that the devil can only come as far as God allows him to come. If he enters your situation, then you know that God must have allowed his entrance so that He could get the ultimate glory.

God gets the glory when the devil comes after you like a roaring lion and leaves running like a dog with his tail tucked under his behind. There are many biblical examples of the onslaughts of the enemy against God's elect, each time resulting in the saints of God having a "demon-busting party."

OH, MAGNIFY THE LORD

I don't like to discuss problems without also talking about the answers. Yes, the spirit of demonic magnification has been released in the land. The answer to the problem is the holy magnification of the King of kings and Lord of lords! Look upon the devil narrowly and magnify the Lord. When you make the devil smaller (in your own eyes), the revelation of how big your God really is can become a reality to you. Psalm 34:2–3 says:

> My soul shall make its boast in the LORD;
> The humble shall hear of it and be glad.
> Oh, magnify the LORD with me,
> And let us exalt His name together.

There is power in numbers, but there is more power in agreement. What if we, as believers, magnified the Lord together? Let us suppose that we could get together and make God bigger! What if we made Him bigger than man, bigger than self or, especially, bigger than satan? In Psalm 69:30 the writer says, "I will…magnify Him with thanksgiving." When we enter into His courts with thanksgiving, we make God bigger!

The first thing you should do is to thank God with a sincere heart. Give God some "real thanks"! Thank Him in a way that is personal and not repetitive. You magnify God when you make your praise personal. You can thank Him for bringing the children of Israel out of the wilderness, but the real anointing comes when you thank Him "up close and personal" for what He has done for you.

God loves to hear you rehearse what He has done for you. The devil is defeated by the blood of the Lamb and the word of your testimony. He is put down when you put God up! When you magnify God, God will begin to magnify Himself.

In Ezekiel 38:23 God says, "I will magnify Myself and sanctify Myself, and I will be known in the eyes of many nations. Then they shall know that I am the LORD." Oh, let us magnify the Lord together, and then let's make it more personal *and magnify Him alone.* Even when you do not have anyone to magnify God with you, magnify Him alone.

I will never forget Operation Desert Storm. I was a staff sergeant in the United States Army. I was newly saved, and God blessed me to head up a Bible study in the military barracks. When everyone heard that we were deploying to war, their hearts grew heavy in fear, and they stopped coming to the Bible study. As the numbers of people slowly depreciated, I continued as if the room were packed.

Finally, only my best friend and I remained. She ministered to me, and I ministered to her, as we both ministered to the Lord. For a few weeks we were on our faces. We praised and worshiped God in an adverse environment. Others tried to spend time with their families or went to the clubs for the last time. The situation grew more serious when the entire post was placed on twelve-hour shifts. Tired and all alone, my friend and I continued to magnify the Lord! My ten-year-old son would ask, "Why are we going to Bible study when no one else shows up?"

But to make a long story short, when it was time to deploy, this young lady and I were the only healthy soldiers, who were not pregnant, who did not deploy to war. I remained in the rear detachment as a supervisor, and she changed duty stations to West Point as a part of the administrative staff. To my knowledge I do not know of any other orders approved to new duty stations during this wartime situation. Normal circumstances would demand that all orders be put on hold during a wartime dilemma. (You can read the details of this miracle in my auto-biography *Against All Odds*.)

It was not that we were afraid to go to war, but we had received promises from God regarding our lives before Desert Storm, and deployment did not fit into the plan of God. I asked God why He had responded to my friend and me in the way He did. God responded to me:

> No one else would believe Me to work a miracle for them
> in such extreme circumstances. In the midst of it all, you
> continued to magnify Me.

We made God bigger than Desert Storm. The people who witnessed this miracle could not believe it. It was an awesome move of God, and it opened an End-Time Red Sea for us to cross over. Because we magnified Him, God magnified Himself in the eyes of the people who were watching. We continued to give Him the glory for the wonderful thing He had done!

We magnify God by faith. It takes faith to magnify God in the midst of trouble and turmoil. I often think of the faith that it took for Mary to believe God when He told her that the Son of God would be born through her womb. Out of all the women in generations past and to come, she was chosen to give birth to Jesus Christ. Can you imagine Mary's thinking? In the natural, there was no possible way to comprehend the facts she had just been given. There was no book she could read to build up her faith concerning what she had to believe. There was no one to whom she could talk who had ever been through what she was about to experience.

When Gabriel appeared to Mary, he told her, "Blessed are

you among women…you will conceive in your womb and bring forth a Son" (Luke 1:28–31). That spoken word, delivered by the heavenly mailman, Gabriel himself, was later confirmed when Mary visited Elizabeth, who greeted her by saying, "Blessed are you among women, and blessed is the fruit of your womb!" (v. 42).

Elizabeth continues her prophetic word to Mary by saying, "Blessed is she that believed: for there shall be a performance of those things which were told her from the Lord" (v. 45, kjv). The word *performance* is *teleiosis* in the Greek. It means that there shall be verification by completion. The blessing is in the believing. When you believe God, He delivers. Mary was blessed among all women, but the blessing came as the result of her faith in God. Without faith it is impossible to please God.

When Gabriel addressed Mary with the announcement that she was "highly favored" and "blessed…among women," the Bible tells us that Mary "was troubled at his saying, and considered what manner of greeting this was" (vv. 28–29). But Mary exercised her faith, shook off her natural emotions and listened to the angel of the Lord as he told her that "with God nothing will be impossible" (v. 37).

Mary had confidence in who she was. She responded, "Behold the maidservant of the Lord! Let it be to me according to your word" (v. 38). Before you can believe God, you need to know who you are. Mary did not look to the natural. She looked to the word she had received from the Lord. Mary magnified the Lord.

THE SONG OF MARY

And Mary said:

"My soul magnifies the Lord,
And my spirit has rejoiced in God my Savior.
For He has regarded the lowly state of His maidservant;
For behold, henceforth all generations will call me blessed.

For He who is mighty has done great things for me,
And holy is His name.
And His mercy is on those who fear Him
From generation to generation.
He has shown strength with His arm;
He has scattered the proud in the imagination of their
    hearts.
He has put down the mighty from their thrones,
And exalted the lowly.
He has filled the hungry with good things,
And the rich He has sent away empty.
He has helped His servant Israel,
In remembrance of His mercy,
As He spoke to our fathers,
To Abraham and to his seed forever."

—LUKE 1:46–55

Mary magnified the Lord, yet many magnify her. Mary never wanted the glory to come to her. She wanted God to get the glory, so she made Him bigger! Not only did she express magnification to God through the words above, but she also made Him bigger in her mind. Mary proclaimed, "My soul magnifies the Lord!" The word *soul* in the Greek is *psuche,* which is related to the English word *psyche* and means "mind."

Mary magnified God in her mind. He was a big God in her mind. Mary was full of Jesus; thus she had to magnify God. She had the Son of God in her womb. When you are full of God, the right things will begin to come out of your mouth. "Out of the abundance of the heart the mouth speaks" (Matt. 12:34). This word *heart* is *kardia* in the Greek. It means "mind." In order to magnify God as you should, Jesus needs to be on your mind. You cannot magnify God when your mind is wandering and wondering about other things.

BE FILLED WITH THE SPIRIT

Not only is it important to have Jesus on your mind so that you can magnify Him, but it is also necessary to be filled with the Spirit. On the Day of Pentecost, Peter was so filled with the Spirit of God that when he spoke, everyone who heard him was filled with the Holy Ghost. (See Acts 2.) They were heard speaking in tongues and magnifying God (Acts 2:6–11). There is no reason to speak in tongues if you are not magnifying God.

John the Baptist foretold of this Holy Spirit infilling. He said:

> I indeed baptize you with water unto repentance, but He
> who is coming after me…will baptize you with the Holy
> Spirit and fire.
>
> —MATTHEW 3:11

The word *fire* means "lightning bolt" in the Greek. When you are filled with the Holy Ghost and fire, it is like being hit by a bolt of lightning. It is an unquenchable fire that burns up and blows away anything that would hinder you from magnifying God. If you are having a hard time magnifying God, you might want to connect with some people who are magnifying Him.

THE MINISTRY GIFT OF THE APOSTLE MAGNIFIES JESUS

The ministry gift of the apostle magnifies the Lord. He makes Jesus bigger in the eyes of men. Never forget that the devil and his gang also want to look big in the eyes of man. Satan would like to control the earth realm, but God wants all the credit for the great things He is doing in the earth realm. God wants the glory, honor and praise. There are many different ways to magnify the Lord, but when you do the greater works of God, He is made to look bigger in the eyes of men.[1]

Paul said that he was an apostle to the Gentiles. Through the works he performed, he magnified "the work of the apostle" in the eyes of the people. When the work of the apostle is magnified, devils are cast out, people are healed, and order is set. In this manner, God is magnified! The enemies of the apostolic attempt to downplay the role of apostles in the last days. Yet there is an awesome manifestation of this office occurring in the earth realm. It will prompt the attention of many, causing God to become larger in the eyes of the church and the world.

The very thing that Lucifer craved has been given to us. He wanted to be somebody. But God took you and me and made us somebody in Him, making the devil to be nothing! God was not *thinking about the devil*. He was not interested in magnifying Lucifer. God is thinking about you and me.

The psalmist said, "What is man that You are mindful of him, and the son of man that You visit him?" (Ps. 8:4). *The Message* translation says it this way: "Why do you bother with us? Why take a second look our way?" But God does *bother* with us—He cares passionately for you and me. You are the apple of His eye (Ps. 17:8). You are always on His mind.

See the enemy as he really is. He was a loser from the beginning, and he loses in the end. God wants you to magnify Him. He deserves all your glory, honor and praise.

Chapter 5

Deliverance
for Me?

I F YOU ARE a believer, then Jesus has given to you the authority to represent Him in the earth realm. You are His agent; as a true believer you represent Christ. We have already learned that, because of his desire to magnify himself above God, Lucifer was cast out of heaven and given authority in the earth realm. Therefore, as God's agent on earth, you have authority to defeat and destroy satan and his spirits when you encounter them on earth.

Mark 16:17 tells us that casting out devils is a sign of a true believer:

> And these signs will follow those who believe: In My name they will cast out demons; they will speak with new tongues; they will take up serpents; and if they drink anything deadly, it will by no means hurt them; they will lay hands on the sick, and they will recover.
>
> —Mark 16:17–18

A believer who does not cast out devils is like a person who carries around a credit card that he never uses. A credit card does not do a person any good until he or she uses it. Before most credit cards are used, they must be activated. A good example of activation is the turning on of a water faucet. The water is in the pipes all the time, but until the knob is turned, the water has not been released for use.

Every believer has the ability to cast out devils, but the five-fold ministry is what God uses to release what is already inside of the people. Ephesians 4:11 describes the fivefold ministry of the church when it says, "And He Himself gave some to be *apostles,* some *prophets,* some *evangelists,* and some *pastors* and *teachers.*" The fivefold ministry is for the perfecting or maturing of the saints.

We come to Jesus in need of salvation and to be released from the grips of the evil one and his lifestyle. Once you are released, the maturing process begins—you begin to grow in God. A sure sign of spiritual growth in Christ is the manifestation of the signs of the believers mentioned in Mark 16:17. But these are not the only signs of maturity, because these gifts must also be accompanied by the fruit of the Spirit as described in Galatians 5:22–23.

As believers, you cannot get around the ministry of casting out devils if you want to walk in the full gospel. Make a decision on this issue, and stand for what you believe in. Deliverance is for you! Unless you believe in deliverance, you are not fulfilling the entire purpose of Christ for your life as outlined in His Word. If you are not a believer, you need to become one and get delivered. Deliverance is not the entire gospel, but it encompasses a whole lot of it!

Jesus came to set the captives free. He could have sat in heaven and loosed fire on the devil's head, but He came down as a *man* and *wupped up* on some devils. He came as an example to us that we, in our fleshly nature, can resist and attack demonic forces in victory. Jesus did not walk the earth as God! He took on our fleshly nature so that we could take on His spiritual nature. The Word tells us:

> Let this mind be in you which was also in Christ Jesus,
> who, being in the form of God, did not consider it robbery
> to be equal with God, but made Himself of no reputation,
> taking the form of a bondservant, *and coming in the like-*
> *ness of men.*
>
> —PHILIPPIANS 2:5–7, EMPHASIS ADDED

He took on our likeness so that we could take on His likeness. There are benefits to being a believer, and they extend much deeper than missing hell and going to heaven.

God gets no pleasure out of watching the devil attack and destroy His children—God loves to see His children beat up on the devil. Jesus came in the earth realm and walked as an example to us. He went to hell, hijacked the devil and gave us the keys. Now He is sitting at the right hand of the Father and watching us to see what we will do with them. God could have saved us and beamed us up to heaven like Scottie on *Star Trek*. But that was not His plan. We are in the earth realm for a reason.

Get a good understanding of your mission on earth. There are some Christians who have their minds so tied into heaven that they are not doing God any good in the earth realm. They are *so heavenly minded that they are no earthly good.* The entire focus of some people's salvation is upon going to heaven. They believe that Jesus took care of the devil once and for all. He did it all!

CAN A BELIEVER
HAVE A DEMON?

I believe that one of the erroneous beliefs of many Christians is that a believer cannot have a demon because the devil cannot cross the bloodline of Christ. My response to this is that they are right! The devil cannot cross the bloodline—*but we can!* If you step outside of the hedge of God's protection, you will reap the repercussions. Ecclesiastes 10:8 says, "Whoever breaks through a wall will be bitten by a serpent." Throughout the Bible, God has drawn boundary lines for His people. If you cross those lines, you will pay dearly.

Some people argue that a demon and the Holy Spirit cannot dwell in the same vessel. James said that this ought not to be so, but it was happening. He said:

> Out of the same mouth proceed blessing and cursing. My brethren [talking to the saints], these things ought not to be so. Does a spring send forth fresh water and bitter from the same opening? Can a fig tree, my brethren, bear olives, or a grapevine bear figs? Thus no spring yields both salt water and fresh.
>
> —JAMES 3:10–12

James was addressing people in the church. He was telling them that he had observed things coming out of Christians that should not be. From my observations of Christians today, I would paraphrase James and say that if a Christian can fornicate, a Christian can have a demon! If a Christian can smoke cigarettes and drink liquor, that Christian can have a demon.

In Proverbs 20:1 we read:

> Wine is a mocker,
> Strong drink is a brawler,
> And whoever is led astray by it is not wise.

This verse identifies the spirits attached to drinking as mockery (to scoff at God), rage, ignorance and deception. James did not play with these spirits, and, as a believer, you must follow suit. In James 3:14–15, he makes his message very clear:

> But if you have bitter envy and self-seeking in your hearts, do not boast and lie against the truth. This wisdom does not descend from above, but is earthly, sensual, demonic.

James identified three symptoms of a person who needs deliverance. That person is:

- Worldly
- Fleshly
- Devilish

Heaven is surely the reward of the righteous, and I appreciate the fact that I do not have to go to hell. On the other hand, *be careful of being so heavenly minded when you have been called to be kingdom minded.* A kingdom-minded person has an apostolic attitude and is not drawn to carnality; he or she is drawn instead to that which causes the kingdom to come!

In order to understand the difference between being *heavenly minded* and being *kingdom minded,* you must first understand the authority of the believer.

THE AUTHORITY OF THE BELIEVER

> Even the mystery which hath been hid from ages and from generations, but now is made manifest to his saints: to whom God would make known what is the riches of the glory of this mystery among the Gentiles; which is *Christ in you, the hope of glory.*
>
> —COLOSSIANS 1:26–27, KJV, EMPHASIS ADDED

What a powerful revelation! Christ in "you" is the hope of glory. One of the meanings of the word *glory* (*doxa*) is "to magnify." When you allow God to use you, He is magnified or made to look bigger in the eyes of men. When you allow "Christ in you" to be released in the earth realm, the devil is decreased in the eyes of men.

The traditional way of living out our Christianity seems to have been just to make it until Jesus comes back "in the sweet by and by." But God is raising up a generation with another spirit. This spirit is an apostolic spirit, and it does not focus on the way things have always been done. This generation has the spiritual balance to dig up the wells of their forefathers and to draw from its inheritance. But this generation will not be regimented to the rudiments of men that were designed to keep people out of the promised land.

THE STRATEGY OF THE KINGDOM

For many, Matthew 6:9–13 has become a carefully regimented prayer that is memorized and quoted just before bedtime or before a sports events in team prayer. But it is more than that— *so much more!* This same prayer, prayed by one End-Time believer, has enough power to annihilate the very belly of hell!

> Our Father which art in heaven, Hallowed be thy name. Thy kingdom come. Thy will be done in earth, as it is in heaven.
>
> —MATTHEW 6:9–10, KJV

There are three focus statements for us in these first two verses of the Lord's Prayer:

- The Father is in heaven.
- The kingdom comes to earth.
- The will of God is to be manifested in earth, just as it is in heaven.

Most Christians are focusing on making it to heaven. Heaven is a security to the born-again believer. Be careful that you do not trust the *natural* (what we see) over the *spiritual* (what God has promised us). A person who has a million dollars in the bank believes that it will be there when he goes to draw from his account. This person even trusts that his account is drawing interest. He never finds it necessary to go to the bank and ask to see actual money. He trusts the American bank system.

As a believer, trust the system of God's kingdom. This system guarantees that heaven belongs to us. It is like a spiritual bank account from which you draw what you need when you need it. As long as you have met the requirement of the Word regarding living right in God, you do not have to keep checking to see if you are saved.

An important part of being saved is having the assurance that you are saved. Know who you are in Christ Jesus and who He is in you! Who you are "in Him" qualifies you for heaven; who He is "in you" authorizes you to do greater works than He did in the earth.

God the Father resides in heaven. No matter how much you want Him to do so, He is not coming down to earth from His throne. This part of the Trinity (the Father) reigns on the throne. Jesus is now sitting at the right hand of the Father as the Great Intercessor. The Holy Spirit is "Christ in us" in the earth realm. The strategy of God's kingdom is this: God's will coming to the earth realm and manifesting itself as the kingdom.

Don't be distracted from this strategy by focusing on when you will get to heaven. Oh, it will be a glorious time! But your focus should be upon standing before God to hear the words, "Well done, my faithful servant!"

"Well done" tells me that there is something to do. In chapter two I listed some of the evidences that the kingdom has come to the earth. Let's review those evidences again:

- The kingdom comes when the will of God is done—Matthew 6:10.
- The kingdom comes if you cast out demons by the Spirit of God—Matthew 12:28.
- The kingdom comes when the children are allowed to come to Jesus—Matthew 19:14.
- The kingdom comes when the last becomes first and the first becomes last (when the smallest seed sown becomes the greatest)—Mark 4:31–32.
- The kingdom comes when the sick are healed—Luke 10:9.

- The kingdom comes when men reject us for the gospel's sake and we have to shake the dust from ourselves—Luke 10:10–11.
- The kingdom comes when men do not walk by observation but get a revelation—Luke 17:20.
- The kingdom comes when the accuser of the brethren is cast down—Revelation 12:10.

All of the above things require action. Jesus said that we should occupy until He returns (Luke 19:13). This does not mean to sit around taking up space in the church like "spiritual squatters" waiting for Jesus to come back. A *squatter* is a person who occupies a space because the true owners have left. A squatter does not have the authority of an owner. He is just holding down the fort!

God is not looking for people to hold down the fort in His kingdom. The church is not meant to be a babysitting business where preachers baby-sit believers until Jesus comes back. This does not serve the purposes of God. Anything that does not serve the purposes of God serves the purposes of the devil. I believe in "black or white" or "hot or cold." Ecclesiastes 3:1 says, "To everything there is a season, a time for every purpose." If there is a time and a season, surely there is a spirit and motive behind every purpose. If God's Spirit is not backing a thing, you can be sure the devil has his hands in it.

THE BELIEVER'S PART IN THE KINGDOM

What is the part of the believer in the strategy of the kingdom? Jesus clearly stated the part the believer has to play in God's kingdom business:

> And I also say to *you* that you are Peter, and on this rock I will build My church, and *the gates of Hades* shall not prevail against it. And I will give *you* the *keys of the kingdom* of heaven, and whatever you bind on earth will be

bound in heaven, and whatever you loose on earth will be
loosed in heaven.

—MATTHEW 16:18–19, EMPHASIS ADDED

In order to get a real understanding of what is being said in
this passage, we must break down the following terms:

Gates of hell

The gates of hell are the vortexes in the earth where demonic
traffic moves from the underworld to the earth realm. The
people in hell are already permanently subdued by demons. They
have no power over the demons. This scripture is referring to that
which is in hell that can affect what is in earth. The gates represent the demonic doorways from the realm of hell to the earth.

You

You are the devil's worst nightmare. Once you discover who
you are in Christ, demons cannot touch you. The movie *The
Matrix* was the greatest example I have ever seen of someone
discovering the importance of who he was. The young star had
difficulty at first with coming up against the agents who were
trying to harm him. This young man could not get a revelation
of the authority he had over the evil agents. However, later in the
movie he became burdened with the need to free his leader from
the evil men. Suddenly he began to believe what his leader had
been telling him all the time.

Now he knew that he was the one called from birth to destroy
the kingdom of the agents. Until that time, everyone else had
been running away from the agents. Believing they did not have
enough power to stand up to the agents, everyone simply ran
away from them. But when the young man stopped running
away from situations that he was called to rule over, the agents
began to run from him. All of a sudden, he had the ability to
stop bullets in the air. He had supernatural powers similar
to those possessed by the agents, but his were greater.

God has given us power over all the power of the enemy. Once you grasp the revelation that you were born to terrorize darkness, you will stop running from situations that are designed to take you out of the will of God. You may not be called to the jungles of Africa to cast voodoo spirits out of witch doctors, but you may need to lay hands on that baby that never stops crying and cast the spirit of torment out. You need to pray that God will give you a burden for setting people free.

Once your heart becomes heavy by seeing the devil hold captive the people with whom you have daily contact, you will have a hunger to see souls not only delivered from sin, but also set free from the demonic control of satan and his evil spirits. There is nothing so wonderful as seeing a person who has been in bondage to the devil set free supernaturally by the power of God.

The keys to the kingdom

The Greek word for *keys* is *kleis*. The verse tells us this: "And I will give *you* the *keys of the kingdom* of heaven, and whatever you bind on earth will be bound in heaven, and whatever you loose on earth will be loosed in heaven" (v. 19, emphasis added). Let's take a look at the definitions of the terms in this verse:

- *Bind*—*Deo* is the Greek word for *binding,* and it means "to tie or knit together." *Deomai* is another Greek word and means "as binding oneself in prayer and supplication."
- *Loosing*—*Luo* is the Greek word for loosing, and it means "to loosen and destroy; to break up or dissolve and make melt." It also means "to break through or to make an opening."
- *Keys*—*Kleis* is the Greek word, and it means "having a key that locks, shuts up or closes."

Based on the meaning of the words we reviewed above, I believe that God was giving us a revelation of the believer's authority over hell. There are two meanings of the word *bind* in the Greek. Both refer to the scripture in Matthew 16:19. *Deomai,* or connecting ourselves to a thing in prayer, is related to the direct confrontation by which God has given us authority to address anything that would exalt itself against the knowledge of God. *Deho,* which means "to tie up like a god and forbid to operate," defines our authority to call a cease-fire when the enemy launches attacks against us. To sum up the word *binding* in warfare, I believe that Jesus has given us power to confront and shut down the works of the devil.

Loosing is actually a type of breaking up. The Greek word *luo* means "to dissolve and make melt." *To loose* is to break up and destroy. As you do this, spiritual breakthrough is inevitable. When we loose a thing, the focus is not on releasing but on making a path or causing a breakthrough. Because the Greek word *luo* means "to dissolve or make melt," we cannot justify declaring or releasing at this point of our warfare. In case you have not discerned up to this point, binding and loosing is a high level of spiritual warfare.

I believe it is important that you understand the mechanics of binding and loosing. The way it has been explained to me before this time is that when you bind something you forbid it to operate, but when you loose a thing you release the will of God in the place of that which was forbidden to operate. In binding, we confront the enemy and forbid him to operate. When we loose, we cause a breakthrough in the spirit realm. As a result, the will of God is released: "Your kingdom come. You will be done on earth as it is in heaven" (Matt. 6:10). The truth is that we pave the way through warfare prayer, and God ultimately releases His will. Please do not misunderstand: I am specifically addressing the issue of binding and loosing. I understand the importance of declaration, confession and release, but none of these refer to this Scripture reference. My military and athletic background helps me to understand the importance of defensive and offensive tactics.

Read the following passages that are often used to teach messages on faith:

> I say to you, if you have faith as a mustard seed, you will say
> to this mountain, "Move from here to there," and it will
> move; and nothing will be impossible for you.
>
> —MATTHEW 17:20

> Assuredly, I say to you, if you have faith and do not doubt,
> you will not only do what was done to the fig tree, but also
> if you say to this mountain, "Be removed and be cast into
> the sea," it will be done.
>
> —MATTHEW 21:21

> For assuredly, I say to you, whoever says to this mountain,
> "Be removed and be cast into the sea," and does not doubt
> in his heart, but believes that those things he says will be
> done, he will have whatever he says.
>
> —MARK 11:23

All three of these scriptures have often been taught from the perspective of naming and claiming a thing or speaking it into existence. We have been taught that we can have "what we say." But I believe that the significance of these scriptures is not speaking our blessing into existence, *but speaking to the obstacle (mountain or giant in the land) that is hindering the will of God for us.*

The problem arises when people are naming and claiming a thing without engaging the enemy in warfare! The true essence of loosing is *breaking up the activity that is hindering our miracle until it can be seen no more.* Though these scriptures do relate to *faith*, we cannot omit the fact that they also relate to *warfare*. Without warfare, there is no faith. The spiritual war we wage is in believing God. Faith is a type of offense (in this case), and warfare is a defense. Any army or team that does not have a defense to accompany its offense will fail at its endeavors.

You make a spiritual connection when you engage the enemy in prayer. You actually come into agreement with heaven. Jesus reiterated:

> Again I say unto you, That if two of you shall agree on
> earth as *touching* [a circuit—connection of things working
> together] any thing that they shall ask, it shall be done for
> them of my Father which is in heaven.
>
> —MATTHEW 18:19, KJV, EMPHASIS ADDED

The significance is that the will of heaven is being released in the earth through our prayer. The keys are given to us to shut up demonic activity. Thereby a path is made for the will of God to be released in the earth realm. Breakthrough happens! I believe that we make a breakthrough by prayer, which opens a space in heaven to connect with the earth in performing the will of God. You make the path; God releases! He brings the increase (1 Cor. 3:7). He also causes the promotions (Ps. 75:6).

You are a trailblazer for the Lord. This is an apostolic term! Jesus was the ultimate trailblazer. He prayed the will of God in the earth realm. He was connected with heaven, and there was a power circuit that loosed a bomb in hell that had a major impact on the earth.

Your mentality has a lot to do with your prayer life. You have to have the right attitude in prayer. There is a saying, "No prayer; no power!" This is so true, but more important than having a prayer life is knowing how to pray right. There is a right way and a wrong way to pray. How you pray has a lot to do with how effective you are in the earth. Isn't that what Christianity is all about? It's about allowing the kingdom to manifest through your life into the earth.

James told his church that they did not have what they were praying for because they were not praying the right prayers.

> You ask and do not receive, because you ask amiss, that
> you may spend it on your pleasures.
>
> —JAMES 4:3

The word *amiss* is a very interesting word. It means to pray wicked prayers that do not include the will of God. Could this mean that the prayers we pray that are not in line with the will of God are wicked? Does that sound too hard? If we are not praying prayers that are the will of God, then we are praying prayers out of our own flesh.

Fleshy prayers do not move the heart of God. Praying amiss does not move the heart of God and ultimately ends up in vanity. Such prayers are useless and futile, and God does not get the glory.

Let us take a look at Daniel 10:7–12.

> And I, Daniel, alone saw the vision [of this heavenly being], for the men who were with me did not see the vision, but a great trembling fell upon them so that they fled to hide themselves. So I was left alone and saw this great vision, and no strength was left in me, for my fresh appearance was turned to pallor; I grew weak and faint [with fright].
>
> Then I heard the sound of his words; and when I heard the sound of his words, I fell on my face in a deep sleep, with my face [sunk] to the ground. And behold, a hand touched me, which set me [unsteadily] upon my knees and upon the palms of my hands. And [the angel] said to me, O Daniel, you greatly beloved man, understand the words that I speak to you and stand upright, for to you I am now sent. And while he was saying this word to me, I stood up trembling.
>
> Then he said to me, Fear not, Daniel, for from the first day that you set your mind and heart to understand and to humble yourself before your God, your words were heard, and I have come as a consequence of [and in response to] your words.
>
> —AMP

Daniel had a prayer encounter. The men with him could not experience what Daniel heard and saw, but instead they fled with fear. Daniel was addressed by a warring angel. As Daniel stood trembling, the angel comforted him and said that his presence was the result of the words Daniel had prayed.

Daniel tied himself to prayer. The angel said that he was

released as a result of the words that Daniel spoke. The release of the angel was the result or final manifestation of the situation. We must see that before the release, there was a war going on in the spirit. The angel was withstood by the prince (principality) of Persia for twenty-one days. The "words" of Daniel about which this angel spoke, *dabar* in the Hebrew tongue, are defined as *communion, conference* and *counsel.*

It would be dangerous to think that the angel was released just because Daniel spoke words in prayer. No, it was more than that. It was the communion, conference and counsel of God in Daniel's life that released the will of God in the earth. Daniel spoke words that were in agreement with heaven because he had a connection with God. It was Daniel's humility in setting his heart and mind to understand the will of God that made the right connection. The underlying factor in the whole scenario was that there was a war going on in the spirit.

Some Christians are so heavenly minded, they feel as though they have no use for spiritual warfare and deliverance. Some people do not want to engage the enemy. However, the truth of the matter is that whatever kind of prayer we pray, whether it is—

- Deliverance
- Warfare
- Healing for the sick
- Prayer of agreement
- Prayer of petition
- Intercessory prayer

—in reality, *all prayer engages the enemy!* Whenever we connect with God, there are dark forces that will be affected. When we affect the dark side, the enemy will retaliate against us. Retaliation from the enemy is a sign that we are doing our job. Weapons will form against us, but they will not prosper (Isa. 54:17).

Just as satan wanted to break the connection Adam had with God when he walked with God in the cool of the day, so today satan's goal is to break the believer's connection with God. Satan is the originator of the thoughts we may have that say:

- We do not need to preach on the devil or do warfare.
- Casting out devils and healing are not for today.

Such thoughts are merely an attempt of the enemy to use those people or to break their connection with heaven. In essence, what they are saying is that the kingdom does not need to come and that it is not for today.

PERSONAL DELIVERANCE

The Bible tells us a lot about how people received personal deliverance. At least four different methods for deliverance are mentioned in the Bible. You may have experienced deliverance in one of these manners or need deliverance in all of them. In any case, *deliverance is for you!* If you are a believer, deliverance is the "children's bread." (See Matthew 15:26.) If you are not a believer, Jesus came so that the captives could be set free.

I do not make it a practice to cast devils out of nonbelievers, but I have witnessed the Holy Ghost take a person off the streets and hijack the devil out of them. I do not initiate the process, but as the Holy Ghost instigates, I let Him have His way. Let's look at each of the four biblical methods for deliverance.

- *Coming out of it*—The children of Israel came out of Egypt (Exod. 13:16). There are times that we need to separate ourselves from specific places to receive our deliverance.

- *A evil spirit coming off of you*—Isaiah refers to a demonic covering that we often overlook, which is the "spirit of heaviness" (Isa. 61:3). This is a false covering that directly attacks our praise. Praise is a powerful tool against the enemy, and he wants to cover our praise up with a heavy deceptive cloak of darkness.

Even after we have received great deliverance, this oppressive spirit comes into the lives of believers to steal the joy of the Lord. Resist this spirit. If you allow it to linger over you, it becomes like a leech that sucks the life (strength) out of you. Succumbing to this spirit makes us prey to a spirit of "false joy." Without joy there is no true liberty in Christ.

- *Cutting it off*—The Bible tells us that if our right hand offends us, we should cut it off and cast it from us (Matt. 5:30). It is better that this hand be cut off than for us to go to hell. There are times when you must cut people and things off from you to get free indeed.

- *A spirit coming out of you*—The unclean spirits came out of the man in the tombs (Mark 5:13). There are times that you must be purged of the contamination of the sin in which you have participated or to which you have been exposed, even though it may have happened against your own will.

The Holy Spirit ministers to each individual as He sees fit. There are no twelve steps or detailed guidelines. For example, there are many things that others have gone through in the process of coming off drugs that I skipped in the process of my deliverance from drugs. The key word is *process!*

The bottom line is this: Let Jesus make you free indeed in whatever way He chooses for your situation. God has a tailor-made deliverance for you. Get your eyes off the method God used to deliver others in your same situation. The way He delivered someone else may be far different from the way He chooses to use to deliver you. The good news is that there is a tailor-made "suit" for you to wear in the spirit that no one else can wear.

The Holy Spirit has counted every hair on your head. He knows exactly what you are made of and what you need. He knows the exact moment that you need to be brought out of a thing, and He will not allow you to stay in it a second longer.

There is deliverance for men, women, teenagers and children. Because of the strategic assignments of the enemy by bloodline, age, gender, race and even territories, God has a strategic deliverance that suits every situation you may be facing.

THE STRONGMAN OF THE FLESH

I am a strong believer in the fact that in order to be an effective deliverance worker, intercessor or any other ministry assignment, we need to be able to "practice what we preach." Paul made this point very effectively in 1 Corinthians 9:26–27:

> I don't know about you, but I'm running hard for the finish line. I'm giving it everything I've got. No sloppy living for me! I'm staying alert and in top condition. I'm not going to get caught napping, telling everyone else all about it and then missing out myself.
>
> —THE MESSAGE

The latter part of verse 27 in the King James Version reads, "Lest that by any means, when I have preached to others, I myself should be a castaway."

First Timothy 1:19–20 tells how Hymenaeus and Alexander were delivered unto satan because they did not hold on to a good conscience and their faith, and thus "suffered shipwreck." I believe that when God tells us in Philippians 2:12 to "work out your own salvation with fear and trembling," He was not just *playing the dozens*. The strongest and most powerful enemy that you have is the enemy of your flesh. No matter how cunning and crafty the devices of satan are, he must have the avenue of the flesh to travel through.

Avoid the shipwreck that comes from sloppy Christian living. Avoid becoming reckless with your faith. In Ephesians 4:19–20, Paul advises the Ephesians with these words:

> In their spiritual apathy they have become callous and past

feeling and reckless and have abandoned themselves [a prey] to unbridled sensuality, eager and greedy to indulge in every form of impurity [that their depraved desires may suggest and demand]. But you did not so learn Christ!

—AMP

Paul continued to say that they should strip off their former nature and be constantly renewed by the spirit of their minds (vv. 22–23). This justifies the fact that there is a clear connection between the carnal nature of man (fleshy attributes) and the unregenerated mind. They work hand in hand together. They are partners in crime, so take authority in your own life to break this ungodly, evil alliance.

It is easy for most believers to recognize satan as evil, but it seems to be difficult for some to see their flesh as evil. That thought hits closer to home! But I will say it again; it is the season for the saints of God to get their houses in order.

Accept the fact that your flesh has a mind of its own. Paul discusses this in Romans, where he teaches by saying:

For those who are according to the flesh and controlled by its unholy desires set their minds on and pursue those things which gratify the flesh, but those who are according to the Spirit and are controlled by the desires of the Spirit set their minds on and seek those things which gratify the [Holy] Spirit. Now the mind of the flesh [which is sense and reason without the Holy Spirit] is death [death that comprises all the miseries arising from sin, both here and hereafter]. But the mind of the [Holy] Spirit is life and [soul] peace [both now and forever]. [That is] because the mind of the flesh [with its carnal thoughts and purposes] is hostile to God, for it does not submit itself to God's Law: indeed it cannot. So then those who are living the life of the flesh [catering to the appetites and impulses of their carnal nature] cannot please or satisfy God, or be acceptable to Him.

—ROMANS 8:5–8, AMP

Most of God's people confess that they want to please Him. But if you really want to please your Lord and Savior, you must deal with and deny the works of the flesh.

In Genesis 6:3, God clearly states that His Spirit will not always strive with man, for man is also flesh. In other words, although God forgives us seventy times seven, even that number is finite (Matt. 18:22). Seventy times seven adds up to something. You must count the cost of sin and recognize that it will eventually add up to death. Scripture says that man "is also flesh," reminding us that God wants us to consider our flesh.

The prophet Haggai advised the Israelites who had returned to Jerusalem from their long captivity in Babylon to "consider your ways!" (Hag. 1:5). The word *ways* in the Hebrew is *derek,* and it means to consider the path of life that you have taken. It also means to consider your methods, mannerisms or how you conduct yourself. To put it in concise terms, it means to consider how your flesh acts out. You are a spirit, you possess a soul, and you live in a fleshly vessel. You cannot deny, overlook and ignore your flesh. It must be sternly dealt with, or it will run the house.

The enemy is battling with you for control of your soul (mind) and your flesh, which stand in opposition to your spirit. This is the reason God wants you to renew your mind, because then your spirit man can be led by God's Spirit. Remember that the flesh has a mind of its own, and it is hostile against the things of God. Anything hostile against God or the things of God is evil.

In my ministry, I minister both to people who have extreme amounts of demonic activity in their lives and to those who have only subliminal demonic activity of which they are not even aware. Personally, I believe that people with extreme demonic activity are much better off that the ones in subliminal cases. The word *subliminal* means "below the threshold of conscious perception."

In Psalm 19, David cried out to God to deliver him from "secret faults" (v. 12). At least the people with extreme demonic activity in their lives know that they need help.

When the Pharisees condemned Jesus for eating with "tax collectors and sinners," Jesus replied, "Those who are well have no need of a physician, but those who are sick" (Matt. 9:12). In other words, He was saying, "If you have not diagnosed the fact that you have a problem, I cannot give you the remedy."

My spirit is grieved when I see how the "spirit of religion" has gripped the lives of many and caused them to hide behind the cloak of lukewarm deception. God cannot use the *sometimes* faithful Christian…the *almost* conqueror or the *hypocritical* spirit that hangs out in the gray areas of life. God spoke clearly to me, saying that He was moving away from those who continually merely *claim* His name. He is pursuing those who desire to *possess* His name.

KNOW YOUR ENEMY'S WEAPONS

One of my goals for writing this book is to teach you about the "little foxes that spoil the vines" and the "little leaven" that "leavens the whole lump" (Song of Sol. 2:15; 1 Cor. 5:6). My aim is to erase the pretty picture the enemy has painted for some on the things we allow to walk with us in God.

Within the church I still encounter people who are uneasy and unwilling to deal with the needs of people like drug addicts, prostitutes and homosexuals. The very thought of a ministry like mine puts a frown on their faces and a bad taste in their mouths. But what puts a frown on *my* face and a bad taste in *my* mouth is saints of God living undercover sinful lives and exhibiting a religious spirit in the church.

The spirit of Leviathan grips the neck of many people to the point that they cannot get enough air to breathe out the words, "I need help!" The Bible states that the scales of Leviathan are so closely knitted together that no air can get in (Job 41:15–16). The word *air* in the Hebrew language (*ruach*) is pronounced *ruwach,* and it means "spirit" or "violent wind." Based on this, it is safe to say that the spirit of Leviathan cuts off revival in a person's life.

Galatians 5:19–21 is a type of New Covenant Ten Commandment Guide. No, I do not believe in being under the taskmaster of the law…do not even take me there! Galatians 5:13 says that we have been "called to liberty," but it also warns us, "Do not use liberty as an opportunity for the flesh." We must admit that there are *dos* and *don'ts* in God. There are things from which we must abstain.

I believe that Galatians 5:19–21 is our warfare manual to battle the flesh. The best way to win a battle is to learn the weapons of the opposing force. In these verses we discover the weapons of the works of the flesh, one of our greatest enemies.

Adultery—*moicheia*

This term literally means "apostate" or "to fall away from your love or initial commitment." When God addressed the church at Ephesus, he accused them of leaving their first love (Rev. 2:4). The word *love* is *agape* in the Greek, and it means "benevolence or charity." Both of these words relate to giving. God was saying that the Ephesians were not giving unto Him as they first committed to do. God wants us to give Him our time, money and, most of all, our attention. The church at Ephesus was distracted by new loves, and the people committed adultery against God.

The word *first* is pronounced *protos* in the Greek, and it means "first in order of importance, or chief of all." Adultery goes deeper than we think. God is a jealous God, and if He is not first in rank in our lives, He takes offense to it and calls it *adultery*.

Fornication—*porneia*

This Greek word is related to the Greek words *porne* and *pornos*. All of these terms refer to prostitution, harlotry, incest and idolatry. It is indulging in unlawful sexual activity that is outside the guidelines of God's Word. The term *to fornicate* is not limited to sexual activity, but it includes the activity of idolatrous acts against God. So to commit idolatry is to fornicate against God. It is to enter into spiritual intercourse with other gods.

We can even commit spiritual masturbation when we act stubbornly, ultimately becoming our own gods. First Samuel 15:23 says that "stubbornness is as iniquity and idolatry." Becoming stuck in your own will and way is an abomination to God.

It is not the inception of sin that removes a person from fellowship with God. Sin must run its course in a person's life. When it is finished, there is a high interest to pay. James describes it so well:

> Then, when desire has conceived, it gives birth to sin; and sin, when it is full-grown, brings forth death.
>
> —JAMES 1:15

Satan has the highest interest rate on the earth, above the earth and even under the earth.

For everything that God has, satan has a counterfeit. He is not the creator, so all he can do is duplicate demonically whatever God has. One of the things that he counterfeits is blessings to the believer. There are two words for *blessing* in the Bible. The Hebrew term is *berakah*, which means "to liberally present a gift." This word is most often related to prosperity. It comes from the Hebrew word *barak*, which has several meanings. One meaning is "to bless God in adoration." The second meaning is "to bless His people." *Strong's Exhaustive Concordance* warns us that this term can also be used in an opposite way—that is, to curse God, as in treason. Satan does not give true blessings; he only counterfeits blessings to manipulate God's people to commit treason against Him by cursing Him with their words or actions. After he has used you up for whatever his purposes are, he slaps you with a bill that will accept no payment less than your very soul. What a price to pay for a temporary blessing!

The second word for blessing is the Greek word *eulogia*, and it means "to proclaim a blessing or to speak well of." The final door to our salvation opens when God proclaims His final blessing upon us: "Well done, thou good and faithful servant." The curses that come with a fornicating spirit will keep us from ever hearing those words.

Uncleanness—*akatharsia*

This term means "to be demonically contaminated and impure." This relates to the infiltration of a foul or unclean spirit.

Lasciviousness—*aselgeia*

This term means "to lack moral discipline or to ignore the legal restraints of God, especially in sexual conduct; to have no regards to rules or regulations; to license oneself to do as it pleases."

Idolatry—*eidololatreia*

This word is related to the worship of images or that which has been reproduced. It is to serve a carbon copy instead of the original.

Witchcraft—*pharmakeia*

This word is related to the English word *pharmacy.* The roots of the professional pharmaceutical business come from the initiations of sorcerers, who used to mix magic potions to heal people. Witchcraft is the strongman in all drug addiction. The term *pharmakeia* means "medication by magic." Satanic powers magically medicate the minds of its victims to alter their moods so that they have no control. The ultimate goal of the enemy is satanic dependency so that the Holy Spirit cannot have His way in a person's life.

Hatred—*echthra*

Echthra means "to have enmity or hostility against anyone; to be an enemy or foe of God or His people for reason of opposition; to operate under the spirit of satan as an adversary." Satan is the god of all who hate!

Variance—*eris*

To live in *variance* means "to live in a state of debate; to cause strife and contention; to always be at odds against any legitimate move of God; to vary with God, His will or His leaders."

Emulations—*zelos*

The Greek word *zelos* means "to strive to be equal with through imitation; to fervently covet what another person has; to be zealously jealous to the point of malice."

Wrath—*thumos*

Wrath causes a person to blow smoke through fierce indignation, or to slaughter for any purpose.

Strife—*eritheia*

This word means "to provoke, incite or stimulate contention, controversy and debate."

Seditions—*dichostsis*

Seditions cause disunion, division and dissention. This word means "to operate in the spirit of the scatterer through dissent." *To dissent* is to always have a difference of opinion and feelings; it is the refusal to conform to the authority that is established by God.

Heresies—*hairesis*

Heresy happens when a person takes a section of the Word and preaches whatever he or she prefers. It is also a religious sect.

Envying—*phthonos*

Envying is to distract through ill will and jealousy (a green-eyed monster). It means "to have a contaminated will unto sickness [this is mostly because of an obsession against what another person has]; to attack through spite." A biblical definition for *spite* is "to maliciously prompt hurt or humiliation toward another to annoy."

MAINTAINING YOUR DELIVERANCE

Getting deliverance is one thing; maintaining it is another ball game. There are many spiritual keys to maintaining your deliverance.

Connection and covering

First Peter 5:8 warns us to be sober and vigilant because our adversary is seeking whom he may devour. Whom may he devour? One of the main ways that the enemy can devour a believer happens when the believer does not have the proper spiritual connection or covering. The word *devour* is *katapinō* in the Greek. It means "to swallow or entirely gulp." This word is related to the Greek word *kata*. One of the interpretations of *kata* is a type of covering or "to be touched." There are two types of covering I would like to address.

1. *Leadership*—God gave gifts (the fivefold ministry) unto the church for the maturity of the saints. The apostle and prophets are the foundation of the household of God (Eph. 2:20). The word *household* is a very important element to understand this point. Household is *oikeios* in the Greek, and it refers to the church family or those who are of the house (v. 19). Individual believers need to be touched by each of the fivefold ministries of the church—including the apostolic and prophetic ministries.

2. *Fellowship*—God warns us not to forsake the assembling of ourselves together; we are called to provoke one another unto love and exhort each other according to Hebrews 10:24–25. Solo soldiers and lone rangers who allow themselves to be separated from the flock will be devoured by the lion.

Separation from the accursed thing

The accursed thing spoken of in the Book of Joshua did not

refer to the things that Joshua and his camp brought into victory with them (Josh. 7:1). They were known throughout the nations as people of victory. They were famous for deliverance. All the heathens knew that they served a delivering God. The challenge to them about the accursed thing was dealing with the spoils of their victory.

The Bible says that you cannot bind the strongman unless you spoil his goods. To spoil the goods of the strongman means to separate from the curses of his territory. When you embark upon things that have been dedicated unto other gods, be territorial in your warfare. In territorial warfare, you need specific directions from God, and you must obey those instructions.

In Joshua's case, God commanded that they not take of any of the enemy's goods. (See Joshua 6:18; 7.) In the case of the four lepers who sat at the gate of Samaria, they were to take of the goods, but hoarding them would cause them to lose their deliverance. (See 2 Kings 7.) When God has delivered you and you obtain victory in an area of your life, you must have an ear to hear the further instructions of the Lord, because there are many more battles ahead. You cannot be an overcomer if you are picking up devils on every level to which God takes you. There are traps on the road to your next level of deliverance.

God takes you from one level to the next level. There are "new devils" on every level. You pass the test of every level when you resist the devil. He will flee! Deliverance is a continual process. God will always leave some things in our lives to prove us and to help us to maintain a "warfare mentality." When you get saved and delivered, you do not join a club membership; you enroll into the greatest army that there ever will be! God is taking His people from a "membership mentality" to a "warfare mentality."

> Now these are the nations which the LORD left, that He might test Israel by them, that is, all who had not known any of the wars in Canaan.
>
> —JUDGES 3:1

Studying the Word of God

"Study to show yourself approved" is a popular scripture in the church. (See 2 Timothy 2:15.) This verse tells us that if you study the Word of God, you will not be ashamed. It tells us that studying the Word will also give us the ability to rightfully divide the word of truth. The urgency of studying the Word is exemplified in 2 Timothy 2:16–18 through the story of Hymenaeus and Philetus. They made an error concerning the truth. This mistake caused them to lose their deliverance and to be turned over to satan.

Their sin was said to be blasphemy. How can a simple misinterpretation of the Word lead to such a serious offense? Verse 16 says that vain babblings will increase and lead to more ungodliness. The words of Hymenaeus and Philetus ate them up like a canker. This word is *gaggraina* in the Greek. It is related to gangrene. When you do not rightfully divide the word of truth, it will eat your deliverance up like cancer.

Breaking old ties and soul ties

Second Corinthians 5:17 describes the confirmation of true deliverance. Old things are passed away, and, when people see us, all things in our lives appear new. Romans 12:2 says to be "transformed" into the image of Christ and not be "conformed" into the image of the world.

Image is very important in your deliverance, because it is what makes you an effective witness in the earth. The image of the world represents what you come out of. The image of Christ represents what you are moving toward. Though your deliverance is personal, it is not just for you! The only deliverance some people will ever see is your deliverance.

Present your body a living sacrifice, holy and acceptable to God. The only way you can do that is to put on the "new man" (Eph. 4:24). The new man will not fit over the old man. Just like a floor that must be stripped and buffed before it is waxed, strip off and lay aside everything that so easily besets you. As you do this, stay away from the thing from which you have been delivered.

> Therefore then, since we are surrounded by so great a cloud of witnesses [who have borne testimony to the Truth], let us strip off and throw aside every encumbrance (unnecessary weight) and that sin which so readily (deftly and cleverly) clings to and entangles us, and let us run with patient endurance and steady and active persistence the appointed course of the race that is set before us.
>
> —Hebrews 12:1, AMP

This passage from Hebrews gives us several important instructions for maintaining our deliverance:

- Your testimony is important in your deliverance.
- You must strip off and throw aside anything that would cause you to fall.
- There are things out of which you have come that the devil is a mastermind at entangling you with again if you do not guard your hearts through separation.
- You must walk out your deliverance with patience and endurance.
- You must be consistent, steadfast and persistent in walking out your deliverance.
- There is an appointed course for you to run.

Guarding your thought life

Proverbs 23:7 tells us that we are what we think. Concerning your personal deliverance, you are only as delivered as you think you are. The overall trick of the enemy is to make you think that you are bound by a thing—when you are not. My strongest bondages were cigarettes and cocaine. After I was set free by the power of Jesus Christ, the devil would literally place images before me to make me think that I was still bound by these addictions.

God's grace was so merciful in my life! I did not have a support group or a mentor who had been through what I had been through. I did not have withdrawal drugs or cigarette patches to help me through. After the devils were cast out of my life, I allowed the Holy Spirit to come into my thought life and take over. God hijacked my mind, and the devil could no longer catch a ride when he wanted to. When satan spoke, it was from the outside! Hallelujah! I heard him from afar because God's voice was so much louder.

We will follow the loudest voice that we hear in our lives. Faith comes by hearing! Hearing activates a thing in our lives. God never said that you would not hear the devil's voice. He said that you would know His voice from the devil's voice and that this would help you not to follow the voice of the enemy (John 10:5). People get confused when the enemy speaks to them. They think that because the devil speaks to them, something is wrong. The devil is a strategist, and he does not waste his time. If he is speaking to you, you are doing something right.

The devil did not tell me I was going to hell when I was getting high in the crack house. But when I got set free, he tried to magnify himself in my mind. After I stopped using cocaine and trusted in the Lord, the devil began to tell me I was still a junkie. He told me that I would never be free. Even when he made pictures of glass crack pipes float before my eyes and made my mouth dry up for cigarettes, I knew that I was free indeed! I had to know it for myself—not even my pastor or God Himself could help me out with that. Jesus had done His part in my deliverance, and now it was my responsibility to do mine.

Take responsibility for your own deliverance! In other words, only you can walk in what God has already given you.

The ultimate part of deliverance is resisting the devil. Once you have submitted yourself to deliverance from God, learn to endure resistance from the devil (James 4:7). He must flee! After the Lord was baptized and identified as the Son of God, He had to go into the wilderness to be tempted of the devil. The angels of the Lord did not come to minister to Him until after He had passed the test of temptation. Jesus was alone during His temptation, and you must go through yours alone.

The devil is not trying to talk you out of what you do not have! The reason he is targeting you is because you have something he wants. You cannot negotiate or deliberate your deliverance with the enemy. It is already settled in the spirit, and it is up to you to make it a reality in your own mind. "Therefore if the Son makes you free, you shall be free indeed" (John 8:36).

There are no *ifs, ands* or *buts* about it. Yes, the enemy will always tempt you with a strange voice. A strange voice is any voice that is foreign to what God is saying about you. The good news is that strange voices will be so insignificant and foolish. Follow the advice of Proverbs 14:7, which advises you to "go from the presence of a foolish man" when you perceive that his lips have no knowledge.

You will hear the devil, and you will laugh in his face in the midst of your deliverance. Do not believe his lies; he is the commander in chief of lies. God will personally deal with the lies of the enemy against you, even those spoken to your mind.

> Thus says the LORD, your Redeemer,
> And He who formed you from the womb:
> "I am the LORD, who makes all things,
> Who stretches out the heavens all alone,
> Who spreads abroad the earth by Myself;
> Who frustrates the signs of the babblers,
> And drives diviners mad;
> Who turns wise men backward,
> And makes their knowledge foolishness;
> Who confirms the word of His servant,
> And performs the counsel of His messengers;
> Who says to Jerusalem, 'You shall be inhabited,'
> To the cities of Judah, 'You shall be built,'
> And I will raise up her waste places."
>
> —ISAIAH 44:24–26

Let me emphasize once again—the devil is a liar! Guard your thought life from him. He wants to infiltrate your purpose with doubt and confusion. Remember that God's voice will not be strange to your spirit man, and He is not the author of confusion. Any voice that does not speak the Truth (the Word) is of the devil.

Moving forward

When the children of Israel were delivered from Egypt, their greatest challenge was coming out of a bondage mentality. Even when God sets us free in our bodies, we sometimes get stuck in that out of which we came. The enemy paints a pretty picture and attempts to get us to only remember the good things about our former bondages. He never allows us to remember the tough times of bondage, because he wants to make serving God seem harder.

We must move forward! Moses told the people to fear not because the Egyptians that they saw today, they would see no more (Exod. 14:13). Elisha prophesied to the people of Samaria and told them, "About this time tomorrow the famine will be over." (See 2 Kings 7:1.) Consider where you are today and where you will be tomorrow. Today moves into tomorrow.

This takes prophetic movement! Because we are a prophetic people who have a word to look forward to, today can never keep us in bondage! Moving forward is a prophetic act. You go forth based on the Word of the Lord that has been given to you. People who are stagnated spiritually have no prophetic insight in their lives. They can only see the Egyptians that they face today.

The greatest aspect of deliverance is hope. Without hope, deliverance is hindered. Jesus told us, "If you have faith as a mustard seed, you will say to this mountain, 'Move from here to there,' and it will move" (Matt. 17:20). Mountains can be moved out of our lives. Faith is the substance of that which is hoped for.

Substance is what fills a container. Hope is the container for our faith. Hope is a foundational word. It gives us a foundation for our faith. In your personal deliverance, your faith must stand trial! The only way your faith can stand is if it has something to stand on. With no hope for tomorrow, how can we foresee ourselves free?

The Lord spoke to Moses and told him to tell the people to move forward (Exod. 14:15). They could not be concerned about the Red Sea in front of them. It took faith for the people to move forward. It always takes faith to move forward.

Lot was delivered out of Sodom and commanded never to look back. When his wife looked back, she lost her deliverance. It is hard to move forward when you have no faith. In moving forward there will be obstacles that will attempt to make you doubt. There will be soul ties that make you want to look back. Always remember that Jesus is the author and the finisher of your faith. He is the one who brought you out, and surely, He will take you in!

Generous giving

Many people do not understand the importance of generous, consistent giving in their lives. Cain was banished with no hope of deliverance because of a hoarding spirit. A true sign of deliverance is that you are compelled to give. Deliverance will cause you to give your best and to give your last. You honor the Lord when you give Him the first fruit of your increase (Prov. 3:9). God likes your first, and He likes your last!

A widow woman and her son were delivered from the spirit of death because she was willing to give her last. (See 1 Kings 17:8–24.) Some may find it offensive that God would require our first and our last. But this is the personality of God—He is the Alpha and the Omega! When you give of your first and last fruit, you take on the characteristics of the Father. God wants us to be givers because He is a giver. Our giving has to be more than releasing finances. Be consistent, generous and strategic in your giving. Give—when God says to give, where He wants you to give and in the amount that He wants you to give.

Deliverance is for everyone! It is for the saved and the unsaved. The first step of deliverance for the unsaved is accepting Jesus as

Lord and Savior. The unsaved person is first delivered out of the kingdom of darkness into the marvelous light. This is a type of transitional deliverance that "brings us out"!

I have seen supernatural occurrences of deliverance to the unsaved. This must only be done by the Holy Spirit Himself. If we make a practice of casting demons out of people who are unsaved, they will only become seven times worse. Miraculous deliverance of this nature is a sign to the unbeliever.

Jesus healed the lame man at the pool of Bethesda (John 5). He told the man, ""Sin no more, lest a worse thing come upon you" (v. 14). Jesus was telling him, "I gave you a miracle. Get your life right with God, or your miracle will turn into a nightmare."

When a vicious religious crowd was about to kill the adulterous woman, Jesus delivered her from the spirit of death. He told her, "Go and sin no more" (John 8:11). Even when God does give a sinner a miracle of deliverance, that person must know that he or she cannot continue in the lifestyle that preceded the deliverance. Jesus is the only deliverer. His ultimate goal in deliverance is for each person to begin an eternal lifestyle with Him. Deliverance is not a temporary fix to make us feel better. In order to be free indeed, you must be a child of the King. It is His Truth that makes us free. Jesus is the Truth!

THE FEAR OF THE LORD

Many people cannot maintain their deliverance because they simply do not fear God. Having the fear of God is foundation for staying free. Without the fear of God in his or her life, a person has nothing to stand on. Take a look at this passage of Scripture:

> The Lord is exalted, for He dwells on high; He will fill Zion with justice and righteousness (moral and spiritual rectitude in every area and relation). And there shall be stability in your times, an abundance of salvation, wisdom and

knowledge; the reverent fear and worship of the Lord is your treasure and His.

—Isaiah 33:5–6, amp

There are a few points that I would like to make from this passage:

1. The fear of God instills us with godly morals.

2. The fear of God gives us stability and helps us not to be shaken.

3. The fear of God promotes abundance of salvation, wisdom and knowledge.

4. The fear of God is a precious treasure.

Deuteronomy 5:29 says, "Oh, that they had such a heart in them that they would fear Me and always keep My commandments, that it might be well with them and with their children forever!"

We need to pray for hearts that would fear the Lord. Not only does the fear of the Lord help us to maintain our deliverance, but it is also a generational blessing. If we fear the Lord, this verse says that it will also be well with our children.

The fear of God has been a foundation in maintaining my personal deliverance. The enemy tempted Jesus, and no matter how anointed you are, he will continue to tempt you, also.

When temptation comes to steal your deliverance, you can make a statement that has helped me over the years: "Jesus, I love You more!"

The true love of God instills reverential fear. The fear of the Lord is a sure foundation. Second Corinthians 7:1 says, "Therefore, having these promises, beloved, let us cleanse ourselves from all filthiness of the flesh and spirit, perfecting holiness in the fear of God." Ecclesiastes 12:13 sums it all up by saying, "Let us hear the conclusion of the whole matter: Fear God and keep His commandments, for this is man's all."

Chapter 6

Why the Devil Hates Women

THE DEVIL HATES women! This is the reason there is so much erroneous teaching in the body of Christ concerning what a woman can or cannot do. The devil wants to keep women in bondage because he knows that women possess an arsenal on the inside of them that annihilates darkness.

Since the Garden of Eden, satan has targeted women. The word *Eden* is defined as "Adam's home." Our homes can still be compared to a spiritual type of Eden. Your home is your place of refuge and a place that has been sanctified unto God. Within the four walls of your home, you can walk with God daily.

Just as satan had a demonic strategy against Adam's home, he has a plan against the home of every born-again believer. His goal is to infiltrate and utterly destroy it. Satan is a strategist, and he operates in dark, deceiving ways. His strategies are most effective when you are ignorant of his devices.

Throughout the Bible and in recorded history it has been obvious that the enemy has launched public attacks against the male seed. Herod released a death verdict for all male babies to be killed during Jesus' era. Pharaoh made the same decree against the children of Israel during Moses' childhood. Satan's attack against the male seed is somewhat of a decoy. It cannot be denied that he has plans against the male seed, but he does not want us to know who his archenemy is by spiritual assignment.

Satan's attack upon the male seed has been a *front-door attack*. Like a "jack man," he has come through the front door to attack males, and everyone can recognize him. He is like the one who jumps in the face of his victims and commands them to lay it all down.

The burglar operates on a different level. He enters through a *back-door attack*. He creeps in through the back door and often attacks in areas where there is little or no light. The spiritual burglar attacks the church in areas where we have neglected to provide the light of sound teaching. He takes his best shot when we skim over the whole truth and leave room for ignorance. Living in spiritual ignorance is the worst darkness a person can ever experience. In order to understand fully why the devil hates women, we have to recognize that the devil's archenemy is the woman. He hates her above all things with a deadly passion. In this chapter you will learn that he is fully justified for his deep-seated emotion.

Have you ever wondered why satan comes against women in ministry in such a pronounced and radical way? The devil hates women because of *what they are made of*. What is it that is on the inside of women that shakes darkness? A popular nursery rhyme says that little girls are made of "sugar and spice and everything nice." But this nursery rhyme tells only part of the truth. God's little girls are made of much more than that.

Genesis 3:15 describes the repercussions to the Fall of man:

> And I will put enmity between you and the woman, and between your seed and her Seed; He shall bruise your head, and you shall bruise His heel.

I want to approach this passage from a spiritual warfare perspective. Where is the real battle in this scripture? A key factor in being able to detect conflict in the spirit is being familiar with conflict from natural experiences. Some of the greatest warfare ministers have some of the most awesome personal testimonies of God's deliverance in their own lives. I have personally been delivered from drug addiction, prostitution, drug dealing and all the other accessories to life on the street.

As I meditated on this scripture, three words were highlighted in my spirit:

- Woman
- Seed
- Rule

Woman

First of all, God intentionally put enmity between satan and the woman. The word *enmity* is *'eybah* in the Hebrew language, and it means "to have hostility or a deep-seated hatred against." It is safe to say that satan and the woman are long-time rivals. The important thing to remember is that God purposely planned for the relationship between the woman and the devil to be the way it is. Though satan is a strategist, he is the subtlest creature of any of the beasts of the field. Yes, satan is the subtlest creature God made, but the power of this characteristic is limited to the terrestrial. His strategies can never maneuver around the mind of God. Satan has a plan, but God has a master plan.

Seed

God put animosity between the seed of the woman and the seed of the enemy. This verse initiated the official establishment of man's relationship with satan. For the first time, satan was identified as the adversary of man in the earth realm.

Rule

A declaration was made in Genesis 3:16 that the husband would rule over his wife. The word *rule* in this scripture is *mashal* in the Hebrew, and it means "to keep order or to be the head of a particular territory." This word is related to the English word *marshal*. A marshal is given jurisdiction in a designated territory.

The assignment of the husband in the family can be compared to a type of territorial warfare. God has given him jurisdiction to rule as the head of his household. As marshal of his home, man is responsible to assure that no laws are broken. If any laws are broken, he has the authority to arrest any rebel that would violate.

To understand fully what God intended when He established the husband's "rule" over his wife, you must understand the word *jurisdiction*. If there were a better understanding of this word, statements like "Women are not called to pastor because they cannot have authority over men" would be wiped from the records. Statements like these are violations in the spirit, and when spoken, they override God's guidelines for man's jurisdiction.

To say a woman cannot have authority over a man who is not her husband and is outside the realm of her home is erroneous. When you submit to this theory, you give men authority outside of the limiting statutes of the orders of God. God clearly stated that husbands were "the head" of their wives. But this does not mean that every man shall rule over every woman. It definitely does not mean that a woman cannot walk in physical or spiritual authority over a man.

God's motive was not to designate *gender* but to designate *spiritual authority*. He set an order in the household according to His eternal purpose. When men attempt to rule based on gender alone, they are territorially out of place.

The truth of the matter is that God promotes whom He pleases. Psalm 75:6 says that promotion "comes neither from the east nor from the west nor from the south." God's measure for promotion is not of an earthly source. I believe promotion comes from the North, the secret place of God. God chooses whomever He deems worthy, and His choice is never limited to gender.

> There is neither Jew not Greek, there is neither slave nor free, there is neither male nor female; for you are all one in Christ Jesus.
>
> —GALATIANS 3:28

Paul addressed the issue of men who desired to walk in the office of the bishop. (See 1 Timothy 3.) There are two kinds of bishops described in the Greek language, *episkopos* and *episkope*. *Episkopos* is defined as an overseer of a local church body. The term *episkope* refers to an overseer who launches out to another level of apostolic authority and oversight. He is a bishop who visits and inspects to give relief. *Strong's Exhaustive Concordance* also calls this type of bishop a superintendent. In the Scriptures, the apostles visited churches to render relief in times of trouble many times.

Who was Paul addressing when he spoke to those who desire the office of the bishop? Because he said that a man must be the husband of one wife, it can be easily misinterpreted that Paul was only speaking to those of the male gender. But the evidence of the truth rests in the meaning of the word *man*. The Greek word is *tis*. This word means "any person, some *one* or whomsoever." The Greek interpretation strongly indicates that this calling was not just to men. Based on what you have just learned, you can boldly proclaim that there is not an assignment or position in the body of Christ that is reserved, by Scripture, for a particular race or gender.

The enemy has launched major assignments against women to shut down the call of God on their lives. Historical evidence exists proving that women have long been considered second-class citizens. At one time women could not own property. Along with the cattle and other material belongings, women were even considered to be the property of their husbands. This is why there are many biblical references to the church taking care of the widows. Widows only had what their husbands left them. A woman as a provider was a reproach to the community. Widows often had to depend on handouts and upon the generosity of others. That is why the widow woman in Elijah's time was about to eat her last cake and die. (See 1 Kings 17.)

When the Israelites left Egypt for the Promised Land, God had to take them the long way around. Although they could have reached the Promised Land in a matter of weeks, God allowed them to wander for forty years because they were not ready to do battle. In Exodus 13:17–18 we read God's purpose for their wandering: "God said, 'Lest perhaps the people change their minds when they see war, and return to Egypt.'" I believe that God has taken the woman *the long way around* for the same reason.

It is related directly to His purpose for her in battle. Though He could have taken the woman the way that was nearer and more convenient, the longer way put war inside of her. Like the Israelites, she may have faced war unprepared and returned to Egypt. A negative attitude toward doing spiritual warfare is an attitude of bondage. You either face war or return to the bondage of Egypt.

The devil hates women because of what is in them—*warfare.* It is the seed of the woman that will destroy satan and his seed (*zera*). God has placed a spiritual alarm inside women calling them to do battle. This alarm is sensitive to the seed (*zera*) or fruits of the satanic realm. Women can sense the setup of satan with fervency. Women have an alarm to identify the seed of the enemy—whether it be a wrong business move, a wrong association or something else out of line with God's will. There is a natural enmity between her and the dark side that demands confrontation. For that reason, satan seeks to destroy the woman of God.

But he delights in using women over whom he exercises his satanic control. One of the most powerful satanic cults in the world is an elite group called the "Sisters of Light." It is no secret that in the midst of high-level satanic activity, there are inner circles that include only women. At any given time, five to ten of the most powerful witches in the United States have been named "the brides of satan."

In Romans 11:29 we read, "The gifts and calling of God are without repentance" (KJV). *The Message* translation says, "God's gifts and God's call are under full warranty—never canceled, never rescinded." I believe these women under the control of satan are using their gifts for the wrong god. Why is it that the demonic realm can easily recognize the value of what God has placed on the inside of women, yet the religious systems of today still try to put God's women on the back burner of silence?

Not only do women have the word of the Lord inside them, but they also have the calling and anointing to do battle. This calling was not as evident in days of old. The revelation and reality of this calling has risen to another level in these last days. It was not the power of the enemy that has held women. It has been a part of God's strategic plan.

Women are more than "sugar and spice and everything nice." The second chapter of Joel speaks of "the fig tree," "the grapevine" and "the olive oil." I believe that this is what God's little girls are made of. The oil represents the *anointing*, the fig tree represents the *sweetness*, and the wine (or grapevine) represents the *new thing*.

When God's girls begin manifesting these things in their families, churches and world, the enemy will be filled with terror. He knows that women will impact their world for God, just as the early church did in the Book of Acts. In Acts 2:12–13, the religious group made jokes about the men who had experienced Pentecost. They imagined that they were full of sweet, intoxicating wine. Peter had to correct them by letting them know that the prophet Joel had prophesied about the exact thing they were now experiencing. He was literally telling them, "This is not *new wine;* this is the *new thing*."

Jeremiah 31:22 says:

> How long will you waver and hesitate [to return], O you backsliding daughter? For the Lord has created a *new thing* in the land [of Israel]: a female shall compass (woo, win, and protect) a man.
>
> —AMP, EMPHASIS ADDED

This new thing that Jeremiah spoke of has a direct relationship with Joel's prophecy of the last days. Joel prophesied that God would pour His spirit upon all mankind. The bondage of the silence of God's handmaidens would be broken (Joel 2:28).

When the prophet Jeremiah stated that "a woman shall compass a man," he was not saying that she would rule over (as to overtake) him (Jer. 31:22, KJV). The Hebrew word for *compass* is *cabab*, and it means "to surround or be about on every side." *Strong's Exhaustive Concordance* gives several action words to describe "compass": close, come, go, stand, round about, remove, sit, down, turn self about, aside, away, back. This simply means that in every way and in every place you look, God will be using a woman. She is His secret intelligence weapon.

We receive an even better picture of why the devil hates women when we look at the three words used for the word *compass* in the Amplified Version of the Bible. These words are:

- *Woo*—"to solicit, to achieve, attempt to gain: to evangelize"
- *Win*—"to reach despite of difficulty and gain the loyalty of"
- *Protect*—"to guard and keep from being attacked, damaged or stolen"

The devil hates woman because it is in her to confront issues that need to be dealt with to win the lost for Jesus. She is like the woman with the issue of blood or the woman who would not leave the judge alone until he made a decision in her favor. What she has come out of strengthens her for what she is about to embark upon. Her tenacity continues to grow stronger. Satan knows that God has put something in the woman to win the favor of her husband despite the difficulty of the season. She will win the loyalty and respect she deserves as a woman of God, and agreement will be inevitable. He knows that the female species will fight for her family, just as the lioness guards her territory to ward off danger.

To sum it all up, deep within them, women have spiritual radar to detect darkness. A wife is the radar of her husband. Proverbs 12:4 says a virtuous woman is the "crown" of her husband. The word *virtuous* is *chayil* in the Hebrew, and it means "an army that is *war worthy.*" This scripture refers to a woman of valor who is bold to do battle. The meaning of the word *crown* is also important. It means "to encircle for attack or protection." It also means "to compass."

To the men of the church, I would like to say: "Men of God, release your women, and allow them to surround you in warfare as God has called them to do. You are the head of your Eden, but your wife is the crown that is called to cover the king's head."

And to all of God's girls: "Women of God, take it from a sister who came out of a lot—*you've come a long way, baby!*" The devil hates you—with good reason!

Chapter 7

Serving—the Key to True Power in the Spirit Realm

THERE IS A great need in the body of Christ for deliverance workers, but there is a greater need for faithful servants. These servants must not only be faithful, but also loyal. Faithfulness is *what you do*, but loyalty is *who you are*. Who you are always has to outshine what you do, because what you do can be tainted with the wrong motives.

Our works can never be more important than our lifestyle. A pastor I know just recently moved from serving his senior pastor for several years to begin a work in another part of town. Someone asked this pastor, "Why did you stay under the covering of the senior pastor for so long when you could have left and started your own church years ago?"

The pastor responded, "There were some difficult times when I could have left, but I stayed because of my love for this man of God and because of my dedication to his vision. I understood the importance of being faithful to get the job done that God had given me to do there, and I knew that my heart must be right toward my senior pastor." His last statement brought joy to my heart. "It's too easy to leave a place when times are difficult," he said. "When times were the hardest, it just strengthened my desire to stay."

Deliverance ministry requires integrity, honesty, humility and faithfulness. But more than any of these, deliverance ministry requires loyal servants. Serving is the key to true power! Many powerfully anointed vessels have come through Spoken Word Ministries. They could look the strongman eye to eye and call down fire, but they did not have a servant's heart. Jesus had the heart of a true servant and the motives of the Father.

A leader who has never served is a danger to the body of Christ. Serving is a prerequisite to power. No matter how high a person gets in position or power, that person needs someone in his or her life whom he or she can serve. As "the anointed in power," you must stay in touch with "the anointing to serve."

Serving keeps it real! When we get so high that we are only receiving service, we deceive ourselves. A person in this state has an ungodly imbalance and a situation that is difficult to keep real. Jesus served unto death, and, more than anything, HE KEPT IT REAL!

Servants breed servants. When people witness leaders who serve, it releases the spirit to serve in them. Take a look at the powerful men of the gospel at the beginning of the church. In their own writings, they identified themselves as *servants*.

- *Paul*—"Paul, a bondservant of God and an apostle of Jesus Christ" (Titus 1:1)
- *James*—"James, a bondservant of God and of the Lord Jesus Christ" (James 1:1)
- *Peter*—"Simon Peter, a bondservant and apostle of Jesus Christ" (2 Peter 1:1)
- *Jude*—"Jude, a bondservant of Jesus Christ, and brother of James" (Jude 1)

As powerful as their ministries were, they were all servants first! Serving is a part of our inheritance. The devil started out serving God from a high position in heaven, but he lost his opportunity to serve. He will never have this opportunity. Therefore, he hates true servants who serve with a clean heart and right spirit. Not only must you be faithful to the work of the ministry, but you must also be loyal to the vision of the man or woman of God whom you are serving.

To be effective in serving, you must understand the role of the armorbearer. God has a purpose for this role, but the devil has a scheme against every purpose of God. Too often, in the church, we tend to look at things from only one perspective. Looking at things from one perspective distorts the overall picture of what is really going on. You may as well gird up and face the fact that you are in a war! You must defeat the strategies of satan if you are to fulfill the purposes of God.

TO SERVE OR NOT TO SERVE? (THAT IS THE QUESTION)

There are five things you should consider before you begin serving in ministry. The answers to the questions below will help you to determine whether this assignment is the will of the Lord for you.

1. Have you been chosen by God to operate in the particular area of ministry in which you are attempting to serve?

> So he departed from there, and found Elisha the son of Shaphat, who was plowing with twelve yoke of oxen before him, and he was with the twelfth. Then Elijah passed by him and threw his mantle on him.
>
> —1 KINGS 19:19

Most people would look at this scripture and automatically focus on the receiving of the mantle. But it is important to note that before Elisha could fully answer God's calling transmitted through the symbolic act of Elijah covering him with his own mantle, there were some details to which Elisha had to attend first.

1. *He left the oxen* (1 Kings 19:20). This represents the fact that Elisha gave up a very prosperous business to follow his calling. He did not think twice about it. When God called, Elisha answered. He did not have any promises or contracts. By faith he walked out into the high calling of God.

2. *He had to kiss his mother and father good-bye* (1 Kings 19:20). Elisha could not put his family before the ministry. In Matthew 12:47–49 Jesus was told that His mother and brothers were *standing without,* and they needed to speak with Him. To *stand without* means to have a need.

   Jesus responded by asking, "Who is My mother and who are My brothers?" Then He stretched His hand toward the disciples and said, "Here are My mother and My brothers!" You have to love your family members with the *agape* love of God. Love for family members in a wrong perspective will cause many to fall in the last days.

   Jesus said, "Do not think that I came to bring peace on earth. I did not come to bring peace but a sword. For I have come to set a man against his father, a daughter against her mother, and a daughter-in-law against her mother-in-law; and a man's enemies will be those of his own household. He who loves father or mother more than Me is not worthy of Me. And he who loves son or daughter more than Me is not worthy of Me" (Matt. 10:34–37). Jesus does not want us to be at war against our family members; He just wants to be first! He does not want us to be subject to the familiar (family) spirit.

3. *He had to be tested* (1 Kings 19:20–21). Review these two verses in your Bible. Elijah told Elisha to go back

to his family in a way that made it seem as though he was not interested in Elisha's service. However, Elisha did not pay attention to Elijah's expressions—he heard the high calling of God. He returned home, completed his business and then pursued serving Elijah.

This incident can be compared to the time in the New Testament when Jesus referred to the Gentile woman who came to him as a dog. (See Matthew 15:21–28.) She was seeking deliverance for her daughter, but He gave her what appeared to be an insult. She saw past the false offense and chose to pass the test, thus receiving the deliverance for her daughter that she sought. Many cannot press toward the high calling or promises of God because of the spirit of offense. The key to remember is that *it is only a test!*

2. Do you *trust* the person you are working under, and can you see the vision?

Now it happened one day that Jonathan the son of Saul said to the young man who bore his armor, "Come, let us go over to the Philistines' garrison that is on the other side."…Then Jonathan said to the young man who bore his armor, "Come, let us go over to the garrison of these uncircumcised; it may be that the Lord will work for us. For nothing restrains the Lord from saving by many or by few."

—1 Samuel 14:1, 6

In this passage Jonathan had a young armorbearer that he requested to follow him into battle. Jonathan told the armorbearer two interesting things:

1. It may be that the Lord will work for us.
2. There is nothing to prevent the Lord from saving us.

These two statements did not give the armorbearer a lot to go on. Jonathan did not sound sure that the Lord would help them. He only told the armorbearer that he knew of nothing that might prevent the Lord from moving on their behalf. Nevertheless, the armorbearer stood faithful with his leader. He responded to Jonathan by saying:

> Do all that is in your heart. Go then; here I am with you, according to your heart.
>
> —1 SAMUEL 14:7

Because the armorbearer knew the heart of the leader, he could trust him. Even when things are not clear, trust leads the way to safety. The Lord tells us, "Lean not on your own understanding; in all your ways acknowledge Him, and He shall direct your paths" (Prov. 3:5–6). True covenant relationship is trusting when you do not understand. When the Lord leads us in a direction that our natural minds cannot fathom, trust is the key to continuation. Submission is easier when the servant knows the heart of the leader. The word *heart* in the Hebrew is *lebab*. This word means "to know the mind or understand the vision of." Any situation without vision is doomed to perish (Prov. 29:18). Armor without vision will surely perish.

In 2 Kings 5 we read the story of Naaman's healing from leprosy. But tucked at the end of that story is the example of Elisha's servant Gehazi, who did not follow the vision of his master but instead deceived both Elisha and Naaman by stealing money and goods from Naaman through a lie. (See 2 Kings 5:20–26.)

I call this the spirit of the ignorant armorbearer. The Word declares that God's people perish for a lack of knowledge (Hos. 4:6). Many are ignorant to the vision of which they are a part. Intercessors must pray that the people will began to partake of the vision of the ministry. After Elisha put his evil armorbearer on sick leave with a case of leprosy, he got a new armorbearer. The only description that the Bible gives of this man is that he was young (2 Kings 6:17).

The young armorbearer rose early one morning to discover that they were under attack. A spirit of fear came upon him. Elisha prayed that God would show him what was going on in the spirit. Servants that work close to men and women of God will see and experience the attack that comes against ministries from an inside perspective. They must have an eye in the Spirit to see the whole picture. There are more *for us* than there can ever be *against us*. But to know this, you must have vision! Fear is the enemy of every vision.

God told Gideon to get rid of all of the fearful soldiers in his army (Judg. 7:3). He told Gideon to "go to proclaim in the ears of the people" (kjv). The Hebrew word for *ear* is *'ozen,* a term for those who are in it for the benefits and hear what they want to hear. This is the opposite of the Greek term *ous,* which means "an ear to hear what God is saying to the church." (See Revelation 2:11.) Leaders need armorbearers who can hear from God. This gift is not to compete with or override the leaders, but it is to be a tool of support and confirmation to them. As the leaders cover the armorbearers, the armorbearers must undergird the leaders. To do this they must be able to hear and see in the spirit.

Elisha's armorbearer could only see the trouble coming; he could not see the answer. Elisha prayed a simple prayer:

> "Lord, I pray, open his eyes that he may see." Then the Lord opened the eyes of the young man, and he saw. And behold, the mountain was full of horses and chariots of fire all around Elisha.
>
> —2 Kings 6:17

Leaders need to pray *personally* for their armorbearers to see the vision. Many have perished because of this simple oversight. They need to know that although there are many obstacles and enemies trying to block the call, *we have more "for" us than we can ever have against us!*

3. Do you *support* the leadership in times of battle?

> And it came to pass, when Moses held up his hand, that Israel prevailed: and when he let down his hand, Amalek prevailed. But Moses' hands were heavy; and they took a

stone, and put it under him, and he sat thereon; and Aaron and Hur stayed up his hands, the one on the one side, and the other on the other side; and his hands were steady until the going down of the sun.

—EXODUS 17:11–12, KJV

There are three key words in this scripture:

1. *Stone* ('eben)—A mason or builder
2. *Stayed* (tamak)—To sustain, to keep, help or follow close (This is how Elisha served Elijah; he followed close.)
3. *Steady* ('emuwnah)—To be the set man; to be stable and secure in office

Aaron and Hur held up the arms of the man of God. When they did this, his position as the set man was secure. Every set man needs teammates upon whom he can depend. The stone represents the foundation of what the church is built upon. Every leader must be rooted in the foundation of the church. I believe this represented the apostolic and prophetic ministries of God. To hold up Moses' arms, the two armorbearers had to stay close to the leader. Based on this reference, it is safe to say that in order for a leader to have the proper support needed, he must have the following:

- A foundation of the apostolic and prophetic ministry
- Support personnel who will stick close in times of battle
- Ministry teams that will stabilize the workload and secure the position of the set man by maintaining their proper positions

4. Do you *love* your leader(s)?

A question you need to ask before you ever attempt to serve a person is, Do you love that person? It is most difficult to serve someone you do not love. It is also helpful to know that as you serve a person your love should grow for them and not decrease. The more you know God, the more you love Him! It is to be the same with other relationships. We are commanded to love each other (1 John 3:11). As we get to know each other, it becomes easier to grow in our love for others.

> For this is the love of God, that we keep his command-ments: and his commandments are not grievous. For whatsoever is born of God overcometh the world: and this is the victory that overcometh the world, even our faith.
>
> —1 JOHN 5:3–4, KJV

Let's study two words:

- *Grievous* (barus)—a burden or heavy load
- *Born* (gennao)—that which is produced from the heart of God

In looking at these words, we can say that anything that is a burden is not born of God. Does this mean that everything that bothers us is not from God? No! But we can say that if we have continued to get prayer, deliverance and counseling for the same situation, and it never gets better, God is not the daddy. It is a bastard assignment, and it needs to be cut off so that we can walk in the real deal.

There is a connection between *love* and *obedience*. God says that if we love Him, we will do His commandments. Instead of praying for the spirit to *serve*, pray for the spirit to love. God has put a natural vacuum on the inside of us—what you love, you tend to serve! When I loved track and field, I served track and field. When I loved crack, I served crack. When you give God His rightful place in your heart, you will serve Him right. When you give your leaders their rightful places in your heart (especially outside of idolatry), you will serve them right. Love covers a multitude of sin. A lot of things we struggle with in ministry can be settled with the *agape* love of Christ.

5. Do you have an understanding of the different types of bearers for the Lord and see where you fit into the picture?

A bearer is one who bears for the Lord. Bearing represents a type of picking up your cross (or assignment) for the Lord. Jesus told the disciples to "take up [your] cross, and follow Me" (Matt. 16:24). To paraphrase it, He said, "Receive what I have called you to do, and follow My example." In Scripture, Jesus warns that any man who tries to save his own life will lose it (Matt. 10:39). He also said, "He who loses his life for My sake will find it."

BEARERS FOR THE LORD

A threefold cord is not quickly broken.

—ECCLESIASTES 4:12

The threefold cord of excellence in which we are called to minister is the call to *lead, serve* and *protect.* The enemy will fight us tooth and nail about these three principles. But in the strength and power of the Holy Spirit, you can lead effectively and bring forth much fruit.

Even though we all have different callings and assignments, we are all flowers ready to bloom in the garden of the Lord. If you want to blossom for the Lord in your calling, learn to endure hard times. Be a perennial flower—not merely an annual flower. Perennial flowers only die off at the top when their roots are deep and strong. But annual flowers die off with the seasons. They are colorful and pretty, but when the cold weather comes, they die with the frost.

Make a determination today to be a faithful servant for the Lord. Serve Him diligently, and give Him your loyalty. Serve those to whom the Lord has sent you. Give of your best to your leaders and to God. Let your roots go down deep into the soil of God's Word, and you will bring forth much fruit in your life. Blossom where you have been planted.

Chapter 8

Deliverance
Testimonies

T HESE TESTIMONIES ARE cases that you may study and
compare to real-life situations that you may run into. All
of these stories are true. Some of them may be difficult to
believe. I have changed details and the names of the people in
the stories to protect their privacy. All of these stories are not
success stories. It is my goal to share both sides of the coin—the
successes and the failures that we have experienced. I pray that
these stories bless you.

PANIC ATTACK (SHARON)

A young lady named Sharon joined our Bible college one year.
She was very bright and seemed to be the perfect student.
Sharon never had any problems, so I rarely dealt with her. She
stayed to herself, and we hardly noticed her presence.

A year after Sharon's class graduated, I received an urgent
phone call concerning her health. She had been admitted to a
mental ward in the local hospital. I was away from home at the

time, and it was a couple of weeks before I could see her. When one of the ministers from my ministry described her condition, my spirit was alarmed. She was afraid to be alone, and her body violently jerked continually.

When I first saw her, my heart became heavy. Her entire countenance had changed. She looked as if she had aged ten years. The hospital released her, but because she required constant supervision, her family considered temporary institutionalization. I refused to accept the verdict that was given to Sharon. I took another minister with me to Sharon's house, and we began to pray for her. Her husband did not understand deliverance or warfare, so we were glad when he left us alone with her.

We prayed, but it seemed as if our prayers hit the ceiling and fell back down to the floor. We began to cry out to God. Sharon's condition had gotten so bad that she had to be bathed, and she could not walk on her own. She was diagnosed with a chronic case of panic attack. The Lord quickened my spirit to pull Sharon out of the bed and command her to walk. She was in terror that if she walked, she would have a heart attack.

Every time she attempted to stand, the devil caused her heart to race. The Holy Spirit prompted me that the elevated heart rate was not real. It was a form of imagery and magnification to make us believe that she was going to have a heart attack. The boldness of Jesus Christ came upon me, and I demanded the young lady to get out of the bed. In fear, she begged me to leave her alone. I pulled her out of the bed and started walking her around the house.

The walk turned into a slow jog. After a while, we ran together as I quoted scriptures and told her in her ear how much of a liar the devil was. I told her that if she was going to die, let it be by believing God and not by lying in a mental institution.

Sharon improved over the weeks until she was able to attend church services on Sunday. Each time she came, I ran her around the church. I told everyone to remember how she looked, because God was going to heal her totally. She walked with a limp and still shook in her body.

My husband and I spent hours on the phone ministering to Sharon into the wee hours of the night. We took turns speaking the Word of God to her mind. One night I fell asleep while ministering to her and began dreaming that the demons were coming through the phone into my body. I was awakened by the sound of my husband's voice as he rebuked the devil. My heart was racing, and I felt afraid. Thank God for the man of God. He was awakened by the Lord to save me out of this situation.

I learned an important principle from this incident: Never minister to people who have strong demonic forces at work in them while your body is tired. I dozed off while praying for this young lady, and the spirits tried to come through the phone into my body. I remember another incident when I was ministering over the phone to an old lady who had seen me on television. The spirit of the Lord revealed to me that she had insomnia and had been sleeping in an upright position for many years. The lady began to magnify the Lord over the phone. I prophesied with boldness, "You will sleep like a baby tonight!" That night she slept—and I did not. I tossed and turned all night. Now when I minister to people with strong demonic forces, I first bind backlash, retaliation and transference of spirits.

What happened to Sharon? After many deliverance sessions and much prayer and counseling, God has totally set her free. She is operating as a communications specialist at a major television station and is a faithful member of my church. Her testimony is a miracle.

RELIGIOUS SPIRIT (CAROL)

We were called to the church for an emergency deliverance session one Saturday evening. Carol had been released from a mental institution and had driven directly to our ministry—a drive of several hours. We were waiting in the parking lot when her car drove up.

What happened next may be hard for you to believe, because it was not easy for me to believe when I saw it with my own eyes. As her car pulled onto the church grounds, the entire car began to shake. A little woman about forty-five years old stepped out of the car. She was talking to herself. As I came closer to her, I heard these words come out of her mouth: "Yeah, Kim can't cast me out. She never dealt with a demon like this before. Benny Hinn can't cast me out; you do not know who I am."

I had come with a deliverance team of five other people, and we had never seen a demon that talked this way before. The voice was totally demonic. The woman was comatose, but the spirits used her body fluently. We were so shocked at what we saw that we sat down and watched as the demon walked around the room (through the woman's body) quoting Scripture.

My husband and I were accompanied by two ex-witches and an ex-prostitute. We were all breathless! Carol's family had been a part of the church for many generations. Carol herself had been in church all her life.

The spirit revealed itself to us as a "religious spirit." We had not heard of such a thing. The demon mocked us and said, "I prophesy and quote scriptures like the Son of God. Everything you can do, I can do better!"

Many people get offended when I mention a religious spirit. Religious spirits killed Jesus Christ. These spirits are legitimate enemies of God. They are "demons of the letter." Second Corinthians 3:6 tells us that the letter kills. There is only one spirit that kills—satan comes to steal, kill and destroy. There is one thief, one murderer and one destroyer. He does not care if he uses a sawed-off shotgun or a brand-new Bible to do his dirty work.

We took a deep breath, accepted the truth of what we were dealing with, shook ourselves and began to work those devils over like a jackhammer. Thank God for the Holy Ghost. We did not know where to start, but the prophetic anointing of God came in and gave us direction. We pleaded the blood of Jesus over that room and took authority over the boldness of the devils with which we were dealing.

The demons began to beg us to leave them alone. We could hear the demons crying as they came out of the woman's body. They seemed to be far away, but the voices drew closer as they exited the woman's body.

God blessed us to be able to discover the entry point for the devils in Carol's life. She owned a house in which no one lived. The demons kept saying, "Wait until we get her back into that house!" The night she had been taken to the mental institution, she had been caught breaking into that house through a window. She cut her body as she crawled through the broken glass in the window frame.

Carol had an ungodly obsession with that house. It was located just two houses down from her mother's home where she lived. She would often run away to break into that house. All of this was revealed to us by the Lord. No one else had given us any information about Carol. Prophecy is an important tool during deliverance sessions.

Carol's mother explained to us that she was unbearable to live with and that caring for her took constant attention. After many hours of deliverance, Carol received a major breakthrough. She is no longer attempting to run away from her home, and demons no longer speak through her. She has a new glow on her face and is living a normal life. The spirit of torment has been broken off of her life.

HOMOSEXUALITY (JASON)

Jason drove to Colorado Springs from another state to attend the Congress on Deliverance held by Dr. C. Peter Wagner. He approached me with a blushing red face and told me that he wanted to be delivered from a homosexual lifestyle. I did not personally minister to Jason, but my team reported tremendous results.

Everything about Jason said "woman." He was soft and feminine, and his physical body took on the shape of a woman, especially in the hip area. We had never seen a man in the church before who exhibited such extremely feminine physical characteristics. If he had been wearing a wig, he would have been the perfect picture of a woman. My husband explained to me that they had to call out graphic things to break the bondage of the devil from this man's life. The session was done in private, and it took several hours.

The result of the deliverance was so effective in his life that his entire family came to the conference the next year. His brother-in-law, who was a gang banger (gang member) and underground rapper (a person who gets paid to rap and curse in foul language), also came to the conference and got miraculously saved. He said that he just wanted whatever changed Jason. He now travels with the Demonbusters as a Christian rapper. Glory to God!

Approximately ten members of Jason's family have been touched by Jesus Christ because one homosexual got delivered. Jason still needs a lot of counseling and mentoring. He also needs more deliverance sessions with follow-up. The good news is that he does not have relationships with men anymore and desires to have a wife and family. The key word is *desire*. When the desire to do a thing is gone, the person has won 90 percent of the battle. Jason now needs to get rid of his "learned responses" in acting like a woman and learn how to be a real man.

LEVIATHAN (ARDELL)

My husband, Ardell, often gives his testimony of how he got delivered from cocaine, nicotine and marijuana addiction. He was also bound by the spirit of Behemoth. (Behemoth is a spirit exhibited by sexual encounters with many women. The Bible says that the strength of Behemoth is in his loins [Job 40:16]. This spirit is never satisfied; one woman can never be enough.) Before salvation, Ardell was a very proud man. He did not answer to anyone. He jumped in his car anytime that he wanted to and drove from city to city, woman to woman, drug to drug.

At one time, I was preaching at a conference at a hotel. Ardell, my old boyfriend from fifteen years earlier, came to see me. He came to the room I was sharing with a friend and asked us to pray for him. But he came with wrong motives—merely pretending to want me to pray for him. The devil made him think that even though we were Christian girls, he could still have a little fun with us in the hotel.

He put his hands up in the air for us to pray for him, and we began to call spirits out of him. We later learned that he began to think thoughts of perversion about my female friend and me as we prayed. Just as he began thinking those thoughts, I said, "Come out, you spirit of lust!" It scared him so badly that he fell to the floor. Ardell knew nothing about the prophetic and thought that I had read his mind. He lay down on the floor and curled up in a fetal position.

We called out the spirit of pride, and he began to choke. His neck blew up as though a bowling ball were coming out of his throat. When he finally got relief from this spirit leaving his throat, he began to cry like a baby.

Although we never prayed for him to be filled with the Holy Ghost, he left the room speaking in tongues. When the demon came out, God filled him. He said that he could not stop praying in tongues for nearly six hours. When his family saw the change in him, they thought he had joined a cult and lost his mind. They were kind of right—he did lose *his* mind, and he took on *the mind of Christ!*

Along with losing his mind, he also lost his cigarette, cocaine and marijuana addictions. Of course, you know, the women had to go, too! "If the Son makes you free, you shall be free indeed" (John 8:36)! God "made" Ardell free when he did not even know what "freedom" was. This story can be found in my autobiography *Against All Odds.*[1]

RAGE (TWO MARINES)

Being ex-military, I understand the regimen and discipline of the training. But marines go through another level of training that I have not experienced. They are taught to be trained killers. People often have a hard time transitioning back into normal civilian life after training of this kind. A couple of ex-marines joined our ministry at the same time. We were having mass deliverance at the church during a training session, and both of them began manifesting in the same manner. They were acting like bulls about to attack someone. They had so much rage on the inside. The spirits in them were very stubborn.

We did not get to continue deliverance. Neither would totally submit to the sessions, and eventually both left the ministry. Both of them divorced their spouses within two months after leaving the ministry. I received calls from both spouses indicating that the two ex-marines had been physically abusive to them, often exhibiting uncontrollable outbursts of rage.

SPIRIT OF THE WORLD

During one conference that my husband and I held, I was supposed to do a mass deliverance service at the end of one of the regular sessions. We had been praising the Lord all night long. As I ministered the Word and was about to transition into mass deliverance, one of the musicians began playing a song that was very much out of place.

This musician had been a member of a very popular, secular

rhythm-and-blues group before he became a Christian. On this night, as everyone looked over at him, I heard the Holy Spirit tell me to break the spirit of the leader of the worldly group off of the man's life.

I called out the name of the leader of the worldly group that the man used to sing for. As I stood on the stage, the musician fell off his chair and demons began to come out of him. He experienced a miraculous deliverance! This was an awesome move of God.

PERVERSION (BRANDY)

A young lady was brought to me by a business associate who attends a very large church. Both my associate and this young lady were members of the prayer team at their church. This young lady had picked up a deliverance book by Brother Frank Hammond titled *Pigs in the Parlor*. Reading the book had stirred up some things in the young lady that she did not realize were there.

At one time, this young lady had experienced a one-time lesbian fling. After reading the book, she began to manifest in strange ways. She had an uncontrollable desire to dance in a perverted way in front of other females. It was not the book that actually made her manifest—it was what was in her, which the truth of that book brought to the surface, causing the manifestation.

The Bible tells us that the truth will make you free. The truth sheds light on the dark areas of our life. Brandy began to feel that she needed some deliverance. She called one of the ladies at her church to come to her home to minister to her. This lady knew a little about deliverance. When the lady reached Brandy's home, Brandy's manifestations were so great that the lady called for help. Another lady from the church came over. When the second lady arrived and saw Brandy's manifestations, she told the first lady that they should leave the house because this type of thing was too great for them to deal with.

Brandy testifies that when the two ladies left her there alone, the demons tried to choke her all night long. Brandy had a history of suicide attempts, and the spirit of suicide manifested itself in her mind all night long. The next day the two ladies came back to check on Brandy. They told her not to pray, but to just go to sleep and get some rest. How can a demonically, tormented person get rest? Brandy had another bout with the devil that night at her home alone.

The women had advised her to come to the prayer meeting at the church the next night, and so she went. After the service, a team of intercessors prayed with Brandy. Brandy's manifestations were like none the people had seen before. The demons made her dance in perverted ways, and she spoke in voices that were not hers. Such manifestations were unheard of in this particular church environment.

But, by the grace of God, Brandy received a breakthrough and was brought to me a few weeks later. Eventually she left her city and moved to another ministry that could walk her through what she was experiencing. She felt forced to leave her church environment, and no one argued about her leaving. Her pastor agreed that she needed to move on. Her demonic manifestations caused everyone to stay away from her as if she had the plague. They thought that there was something wrong with Brandy.

How many other people have demons inside them that have been kept at bay? But because Brandy wanted deliverance, she got it.

Over the years, I have learned that we can keep as many demons as we want to keep. The situation with Brandy reminds me of the response of the people after Jesus cast the demons into the swine. (See Mark 5:1–20.) The people sent word to Jesus advising Him *not* to come to their town. They closed up their pigpens and kept Him out. Always remember that you can keep as many demons as you would like! If you close your pen to

Jesus, He will allow you to keep your pigs in your parlor. Let's take a look at what the Bible says about this account:

> So those who fed the swine fled, and they told it in the city and in the country. And they went out to see what it was that had happened. Then they came to Jesus, and saw the one who had been demon-possessed and had the legion, sitting and clothed and in his right mind. And they were afraid. And those who saw it told them how it happened to him who had been demon-possessed, and about the swine. Then they began to plead with Him to depart from their region.
> —Mark 5:14–17

Brandy was treated in a different way after she was delivered. People were afraid of what she had gone through. The trauma of hearing demons speak through her body was enough to have to deal with, but she also had to deal with the "rejection due to ignorance."

God tells us that His people perish for lack of knowledge. We must provide deliverance for the people and a place for them to feel safe after they have been delivered. In Mark 5:16, the man delivered from the spirit of Legion wanted to follow Jesus, but Jesus would not allow him to go with Him. He told him to stay and witness to the ones who knew what he came out of.

This was not the case with this young lady, but it is ideal to have a local church base from which people can get delivered *and* mentored.

TRANSFERENCE OF SPIRITS (JANICE)

A young lady brought her daughter to one of our services. The service was good, but it was a usual service with nothing outstanding to talk about. They came up to me after the service, and her daughter had on some jewelry that made me feel very uncomfortable.

The young lady told me that she wanted prayer, but that I was the only one who could lay hands on her. I was concerned about her motives and asked her why. She said that she was a minister and was trying to get back to God. She explained that she was a part of a church that practiced the laying on of hands, and she believed spirits had been transferred to her. She said a man had posed as an apostle, but he was later found to be living a lifestyle contrary to that; she left God on that account.

I do not make it a practice to pray for people who want only me to pray for them for two reasons:

1. That person could be a witch with the wrong motives who simply wants to make contact with me.
2. My goal is to teach people not to be form an idolatrous dependency on a spiritual leader. Jesus is the healer. Unless there is a specific revelation from God that a particular person must pray for another person, we should be open to allow the Holy Spirit to use whomever He chooses. Even with this, motives should be right, and we should keep our hearts clear of idolatry.

However, the Lord gave me a confirmation that I was to pray for this woman. As I began to lay hands on her, I could sense that there were spirits in the form of people standing around her. I said, "You have people following you in the spirit! They curse you, but they came in the name of Jesus."

When I said that, these people tried to open a third eye in her head. I touched her forehead, and she was slung violently about fifteen feet from where she had been standing before me. She began crawling on the floor like a wild animal. She had a spirit of fear on her face that I will never forget. I knew that these manifestations were the result of a voodoo curse.

Every time I reached my hands toward her, she would be supernaturally thrown five to ten feet away from me. This began at the pulpit and ended at the entrance of the church. My deliverance workers all agree that this was one of the most unbelievable demonic manifestations we have ever witnessed. Words cannot describe what we saw that night.

I can tell you that the voodoo spirits left her body with a screeching scream. She was supernaturally set free by the power of God as her body fell limp with relief. To God be the glory!

For more information on transference of spirits, read chapter eleven.

Physical Healing

When Paul anointed handkerchiefs for the sick, the diseases departed from the people and evil spirits went out from them (Acts 19:11–12). It is no secret that there is a direct relationship between deliverance and healing. We learn in these verses that the disease and the demons left at the same time.

Can we say that all sickness is caused by a demon? If I have influenza, does this mean that I have a devil? The best way to explain it is to look at the source. If Jesus is the healer, then satan is the one that causes sickness. It is the source that counts! Jesus came that we might have abundant life, but satan comes to steal, kill and destroy.

I believe that all sickness is a result of demonic attack, but it does not mean that the person is in sin. We do not have to do wrong for doors of infirmity to open in our life. Infirmity is defined as a spirit in the Bible. We open ourselves to spirits when we do not obey the Word of God, but the devil also sends attacks against us, especially when we are doing right. Though the manifestation is physical, the root of sickness is supernatural.

Therefore, to get to the root of our healing, it must be supernatural. I realize that we have to use natural means to reach healing at times. But without God's involvement, healing will not take place. God gave us surgeons with hands of precision to operate on us, but we still need His blessing. If He does not blow on it, the surgeon's expertise will be null and void.

When there is no natural skill or knowledge, the Holy Spirit can use anybody He pleases. God uses me in this way a lot. I believe myself to be a person who is not knowledgeable or skilled in a lot of areas. That which I know, I have no problem activating and making it work. On the other hand, I do not like to crowd my mind with things that I do not "need to know." There are things like medical issues, investments and archaeology that I choose not to go out of my way to learn about until it is necessary.

Yet these are the areas where God uses me in the mightiest ways—the areas that I know nothing about! When that happens, there is no doubt that "it is all Him."

Recently the Lord allowed me to experience two healing miracles in one day. I was at a place of business and noticed a woman who had a peculiar look on her face. I know it must have been supernatural, because I noticed her face from a distance as I walked down the hall. She told me that she had Bell's palsy and had been suffering for several years. At the end of the workday we met in her office. One of the office personnel stayed with my husband and me as we prayed for her. As we began to call the spirits of death, infirmity and paralysis out of her, her face began to distort. Her mouth opened wide, and she began to groan. When everything was done, she had feeling in her face for the first time in years.

Before prayer, she could only open her mouth slightly and could not blink one eye. Now she can blink her eye and open her mouth wide. As she plucked her eyebrow on the side of her face that was attacked, she could feel the pain. God restored her natural beauty, and she no longer suffered from the numbness of this demonic attack.

Later that night, I gave the young man a ride home after he helped me to minister to the woman with Bell's palsy. His mother-in-law was at his home when we arrived. She asked me to pray for her, and my husband immediately began breaking spirits off of her. God gave me a word of knowledge that something was wrong in her chest. We prayed for her, and later discovered that she had been diagnosed with a possible hole in her heart.

This occurred around 9:30 P.M. At 2:00 A.M. the same woman was taken to the emergency room with a heart attack. When I was alerted, the first thing I remembered was that God had given me a word of knowledge. I thought, *God would not bring anything up that He was not going to deal with!*

The woman was in her early fifties, but she looked young and seemed to be in very good shape. The family was preparing for the worst—heart surgery. We began to intercede on behalf of the woman and to thank God for her healing. When they tested her a few days later, *there was no hole!*

Jesus is the Master Surgeon. Sometimes it gets worse before it gets better, but God is never too late. He is always right on time.

Chapter 9

The Ministry of Jesus Christ

THE MINISTRY OF Jesus Christ falls under three categories. These categories are life, labor and love. My slang for it is "blood, sweat and tears." Review the following chart for a better understanding of these categories:

THE MINISTRY OF JESUS CHRIST

Life	**Blood**	Jesus came so that we could have abundant life. He died a harsh death so that we could have high life (John 10:10).
Labor	**Sweat**	Jesus labored in the Garden of Gethsemane until the job was finished. He labored unto death (Matt. 26:38).
Love	**Tears**	When Jesus ministered to the crowds, He was moved with compassion.

> Jesus wept when Lazarus died, and
> the people witnessed how much He
> loved him (John 11:35–36).

These three attributes make up the ministry of Jesus Christ. Scripture tells us that there is life in the blood (Gen. 9:4). In order for us to live, Jesus had to die! John 15:13 says, "Greater love has no one than this, than to lay down one's life for his friends."

The natural heart is the determining factor for natural life. If the heart is not working properly, a person cannot live a full life. Jesus had a heart of pure gold. He ministered with power and authority, yet the people saw His heart. Jesus' public ministry was not just a front. He allowed the people to see who He really was. He cried when Lazarus died. He chased the moneychangers out of the temple when He was mad. Jesus also rejoiced and thanked God for hiding revelation from the wise and giving it to the babes in Christ (Luke 10:21).

Jesus kept it real. He hated hypocrites. The Scriptures show that He would bust them out every now and then:

> Hypocrites! Well did Isaiah prophesy about you, saying:
> "These people draw near to Me with their mouth, and
> honor Me with their lips; but their heart is far from Me."
> —Matthew 15:8

If Jesus kept it real, I believe that it is important that we keep it real. What is the first step in keeping it real? Pray a prayer like the one David prayed:

> Create in me a clean heart, O God; and renew a right spirit
> within me.
> —Psalm 51:10, KJV

David prayed for a "clean heart" and a "right spirit." The two actually walk hand in hand. I believe that a clean heart produces a right spirit.

Deliverance ministry was a very important part of the ministry of Jesus Christ. But before we plunge into the depths of the deliverance ministry of Jesus, we must deal with the prerequisites. True power over unclean spirits comes by not allowing them to have a part of your heart. Our heart determines our quality of life. The quality of life that we live affects our ability to be effective in our labor. This is truth whether you are someone who wants to help someone else get delivered, or if you are the one who desperately needs deliverance.

In either case, you will have to consider the state of your heart. Our dedication to labor is a spiritual gauge that determines the "genuineness" of our love. May I ask you a question? How real is your love? How real is your love for others, but first of all, how real is your love for yourself? The true strength of Jesus' ministry was His love!

Love only operates fluently through a clean heart. Clean hearts promote clear consciences. The main tactic of the enemy is to instill fear when it comes to true deliverance. The Word of the Lord says, "God has not given us a spirit of fear, but of power and of love and of a sound mind" (2 Tim. 1:7).

There it is again…the connection between power and love! I am so glad that a sound mind is a part of this threefold cord also. To have a "sound mind" means to be sober. The only way that we can be vigilant is to be sober. The devil does not play fair, and he loves to send bombardments of imagery and magnification to distract us from our purpose. Whether you purpose to read this book in order to get free yourself or to help someone else to get free, always remember to stick to the purpose.

Jesus never let circumstances or situations distract Him from His purpose. The assignment of the religious group that attacked Jesus' ministry was to distract Him from His purpose. This assignment has not changed today. Religious spirits have been enemies of true deliverance ministries for a long time. These spirits are even more prevalent today. When the religious crew accused Jesus of casting out devils by Beelzebub, He ended His response to them with this statement: "He who is not with Me [in this ministry] is against Me" (Luke 11:23).

This is where the line is drawn in the spirit. Yes, a line has been drawn, and Jesus was the one who drew it. Born-again believers have often made the mistake of making deliverance ministry an option. In this scripture in Luke, He described two kinds of people. He was talking about the ones who *scattered* and the ones who *gathered.*

Jesus was discussing satan, Beelzebub and the strongman in Luke 11:14–22. In the next verse Jesus said, "He who is not with Me is against Me" (v. 23).

Then in verse 24, Jesus began talking about unclean spirits walking through dry places and seeking rest. Jesus was speaking about deliverance before and after verse 23. Did Jesus bump His head and start talking crazy in verse 23? No! When He addressed the issue of people either being for or against Him, He was refer-ring to *people supporting or coming up against Him in deliverance ministry.* This is where the line is drawn!

Will we really pick up this cross and follow Jesus? Deliverance ministry *was, is* and *will always be* the ministry of Jesus Christ. Jesus is the same yesterday, today and forevermore. My spirit man rejoices when I think about it!

Jesus told us that there would be signs that follow true believers.

> And these signs will follow those who believe: In My name they will cast out demons; they will speak with new tongues; they will take up serpents; and if they drink any-thing deadly, it will by no means hurt them; they will lay hands on the sick, and they will recover.
>
> —Mark 16:17–18

The enemy has deceived many believers into running after

signs. Jesus told the Pharisees that it was wicked to run after a sign. We should not run after signs. Scripturally speaking, *the signs should be running after us!* When we put devils on the run, the signs and wonders will run us down and take us over. I do not believe in looking for devils under every bush. On the other hand, I do believe that if a devil lifts its head, we have been given power and authority to cut it off.

It is not enough to tear down strongholds; we must cast out devils. We have been doing spiritual warfare with no follow-up in the church. The follow-up is the ministry of casting out devils. It does not make sense to go up to the high places if we are not going to deal with the strongman when we get there. Scripture clearly reveals that when we bind up the strongman, we can spoil his goods. This word *goods* is *skeuos* in the Greek, and it refers to his equipment, apparatus or that which is useful to him.

The Bible says that the wealth of the wicked is stored up for the just (Prov. 13:22). When you jack the strongman, you get his stuff! You have access to the same stuff he has been using to destroy our marriages, churches, children and businesses.

Let me give you an example. The enemy has been using the music of the world to take the hearts of our young people from Jesus. When you walk in the authority of your right to spoil the goods of the strongman in this area, you can take the same tool that the enemy used for his glory and use it for the glory of God's kingdom.

The key is in understanding how to spoil the enemy's goods. Luke said, "When a strong man, fully armed, guards his own palace, his goods are in peace" (Luke 11:21). We must jack (hijack) the enemy of his goods (apparatus). The word *spoil* in Matthew 12:29 is *diarpazo* in the Greek, meaning "to seize and plunder." Deliverance ministry is the highest level of spiritual warfare. It is when the foot soldiers of the Lord confront the enemy one on one. It is the key to disarming the enemy and stripping him of all rights to operate in the area that he has attacked. Deliverance ministry puts an end to the enemy's bondage in an area. We have the promise of God that "He will make an utter end of it. Affliction will not rise up a second time" (Nah. 1:9).

The presence of Jesus disarmed demons. I believe that God's anointing upon you can be so strong that demons will cry out when you come on the scene. Your presence should demand respect from the demonic. Why? Because you have Jesus on the inside of you—when you show up, devils must flee. When Jesus entered the synagogue, the devils screamed, "Let us alone! What have we to do with You, Jesus of Nazareth?" (Mark 1:24).

The devils had no part in Jesus. Because Jesus had no communion with darkness, He could walk in the power of the light. Demons hate the light. They want your goodness to be evil spoken of. They desire that the light in you become darkness. The greatest power that we can ever walk in is a lifestyle that is pleasing to the Lord.

When we get into tough situations, I do not believe it is wise to walk around with a question mark over our heads, asking, "Hmmm, what would Jesus do?" I believe that we should have an exclamation mark over our heads—and simply do what Jesus did! He stepped down out of glory and walked as a man in the earth realm to be the perfect example. As true disciples, we should "do what Jesus did!"

A major portion of Jesus' ministry was casting out devils. The importance of casting out devils does not rest in the fact that something leaves the person when the devils are cast out. The importance is not *what is leaving;* it is *what is coming in.* Jesus made this point in Matthew 12:28 when he said, "If I cast out demons by the Spirit of God, *surely the kingdom of God has come upon you*" (emphasis added). Luke 11:20 says, "If I cast out demons with the finger of God, surely the kingdom of God has come upon you." This tells us two things. We are vessels being used for His glory, but it is:

- By God's finger
- By God's Spirit

This is an interesting point. I believe that its purpose is to remind us to keep the focus on Jesus. Jesus is the deliverer! Jesus gave us a perfect example by keeping His focus on God. He often reminded His followers that He came to do the work of His Father. Jesus was a "sent one." He is the perfect example of the apostolic. The apostolic ministry of Christ is a pioneering, spearheading ministry that lays out the pattern for many to follow. The apostolic is a fathering spirit. Every good father desires to see his children accomplish more than he did. Jesus left an inheritance that every born-again believer should take advantage of. Jesus prophesied that we would do greater works than He did.

> For the Father loves the Son, and shows Him all things that He Himself does; and He will show Him greater works than these, that you may marvel. For as the Father raises the dead and gives life to them, even so the Son gives life to whom He will.
>
> —JOHN 5:20–21

> He who believes in Me, the works that I do he will do also; and greater works than these he will do, because I go to My Father.
>
> —JOHN 14:12

According to these verses, the prerequisites to receiving the inheritance that Jesus left to us, enabling us to do the greater works, are:

1. To be a believer
2. To be a son

The sons of God are led by His Spirit. Submission is the key! James told us to "submit to God. Resist the devil and he will flee from you" (James 4:7). Submission opens the door to casting the devil out. Without submission, demons have territorial rights to stay! Jesus showed the ultimate example of submission to God.

Hebrews 12:1 warns us to "lay aside every weight, and the sin which so easily ensnares us." One of the meanings of this phrase is to be pulled in every direction. We must separate ourselves from anything that would pull us off course. Disobedience puts us off course. Jesus' ministry was right on time—He stayed on track and in tune with the Father. This will be the End-Time sign of the true believer. As a true believer, you will say what God says and do what Jesus did!

When we stand with Jesus in deliverance ministry, we are standing with ministry in its entirety. To be Christlike is to cast out devils. Will you stand with Jesus in the ministry of casting out devils? Will you gather or scatter?

When people come up against deliverance ministry out of ignorance, they scatter the flock. Deliverance ministry "draws things together." It is the missing link in the minds of men. It is the answer when we just cannot get it together. Deliverance brings closure to our loose ends.

Have you fasted and prayed to no avail? Have you read the Word and quoted the Scriptures until you can do so no longer? If you have done all of the above and have no other options, you may want to consider this aspect of the ministry of Jesus Christ. If there is an area in your life that has been broken down by the demonic, allow the chief demon buster, Jesus Christ, to set you free. First John 3:8 says that it was for this purpose that the Son of God was manifested, that He might destroy the work of the devil! Have this confidence—whom the Son makes free is free indeed. If you have a *devil problem,* then you need a *Jesus answer!*

Chapter 10

General Guidelines for Effective Deliverance Work

FROM READING THE previous chapters to this book, you have learned several important things about deliverance ministry. In this chapter I will give you some guidelines for doing deliverance ministry effectively. But first, let's review some of the important things you have already learned:

- Jesus came to set the captives free.

- The process of becoming new involves *reconciliation, restoration* and *transformation.*

- We must separate fully from the spiritual afterbirth of our new birth experience.

- We should identify the strongman by name.

- Satan operates through magnification and imagery.

- When we bind ourselves to heaven in prayer and forbid the operation of darkness, the will of God is released in the earth realm.

- The enemy has launched major assignments against women to shut down the call of God on their lives.

- God desires that we serve Him as loyal armorbearers.

- Deliverance brings closure to our loose ends.

By keeping these principles in mind, we can now move forward by learning the guidelines to effective deliverance ministry.

GUARD YOUR THOUGHT LIFE

Demons will impersonate God in your thoughts. Satan himself masquerades an as angel of light (2 Cor. 11:14). Demon spirits attempt to make us think more highly of ourselves than we ought to (Rom. 12:3). They try to flatter us with lies that trick us into exalting ourselves against the knowledge of God (2 Cor. 10:5).

In 2 Corinthians 10:5 Paul reminds us that our weapons are mighty for "casting down imaginations, and every *high thing* that exalteth itself against the knowledge of God." The Greek term for the phrase *high thing* is *hupsoma*. *Hupsoma* means "elevated person, place or thing." *Hupsoma* is the reason that Lucifer was kicked out of heaven.

It feels good to be used by God. It feels even better to see a person who is bound by the demonic set free. The enemy will always attempt to make the deliverance worker think that the success for the deliverance of another person rests in his or her intervention. As we begin to work in a deliverance ministry, we must develop the same attitude we see in Joseph when Pharaoh asked him to interpret his dream. Joseph responded, "It is not in me; God will give Pharaoh an answer" (Gen. 41:16). So it is with deliverance ministry. It is not in us (alone) to do it, but our God will deliver!

If the enemy cannot get the worker to exalt himself in his own mind, he will attempt to turn the workers against each other. The enemy does this through imagery, magnification and confusion. Extreme spirits of insecurity, jealousy, competition and pride easily open the door to disunity. These spirits must be recognized and dealt with.

Do Not Be Intimidated
by Demonic Threats

Demons will often attempt to instill fear in the hearts and minds of the workers. Know God and the authority that He has given you.

Some time ago, my husband and I were ministering to a young lady who had some serious psychological issues. This sister had not combed her hair in quite some time. It was matted to her head. As we began to cast devils out of her before a crowd of about one thousand people, the devils tried to distract us from the deliverance by fear tactics. The young girl started pulling handfuls of hair from her head. It looked painful and frightful. The demon-possessed girl ran toward me and put her hands around my neck to choke me. Only inches from my neck, her hands could not close to touch my skin. This was a supernatural manifestation of God's protection. The girl growled and struggled to close her hands to no avail.

This was one day that I was glad that I was not one of the seven sons of Sceva. Hallelujah! The enemy can never touch you as long as you do not play his game. His game is sin. Give no room to the enemy!

Understand the Territorial
Restrictions of the Enemy

Satan's influence is restricted to the parameters God has set. God promises us victory according to the coast that He has given us.

> Every place that the sole of your foot will tread upon I have given you, as I said to Moses. From the wilderness and this Lebanon as far as the great river, the River Euphrates, all the land of the Hittites, and to the Great Sea toward the going down of the sun, shall be your territory [coast]. No

man shall be able to stand before you all the days of your
life; as I was with Moses, so I will be with you. I will not
leave you nor forsake you.

—Joshua 1:3–5

Many people misinterpret this scripture to indicate that
wherever the sole of their feet touch, that land will belong to
them. They leave out a few important words: In the King James
Version, verse 4 reads "shall be your coast." God had just given
very specific geographical descriptions of the boundaries of that
"coast." He told them that their battles would be successful when
they were fought within those boundaries.

When you fight battles that God has not called you to fight,
you will surely be taken out by territorial spirits. As long as you
operate within the boundaries of your assigned coast, God
promises that no enemies will stand before you.

Satan is a created and fallen creature. He is a murderer and a
liar, the father of lies (John 8:44). He is the craftiest creature that
God has ever made. He is not omnipresent or omniscient. He is
most certainly not omnipotent. He roams around seeking
whom He may devour. There are many ways that devouring
spirits operate, but the main way is to get a person territorially
out of place. If the wolf can pull one of the sheep away from the
rest of the flock, the sheep is doomed for destruction.

IMPORTANT CONSIDERATIONS WHEN
DEALING WITH DEMONIC SPIRITS

There are two very important points to remember when you are
dealing with demonic spirits. First is that they are able to hide
in the flesh and to make people think their problems are natural. But second, as a believer confronts them with wisdom,
experience and the prophetic anointing, the demons can be
forced to expose their presence, assignment and point of origin.

As you confront the demonic, you can have a confirmation

that a particular spirit is actually *present*. You can also determine the *actual assignment* that spirit has received against that person. And you can also find out the *point of origination* that opened the door for that spirit to enter.

Demonic presence

Many times we are tricked into believing that a person does not need deliverance because of the absence of manifestations. The absence of manifestations does not mean that no demons are present. Many times demons will become so familiar with the person that they hide in the flesh of that person and pretend to be the person. We are often trapped into calling some things *habits* that are actually demons.

Demons can be so suppressed in the life of a person that they are unrecognizable. I know a minister who always hoarded everything. He stockpiled things as though a war was coming soon and he would be locked in the cellar. Everyone noticed his fear of sharing what he considered to be "his." Out of ignorance everyone overlooked what they thought was "just him."

But some time later he walked away from his calling. He began to make statements like, "My life is almost over, and I have nothing to show for it." The spirit of greed took this brother out. What we had excused as "just him" was actually a hoarding demon that had opened the door to an uncontrollable spirit of greed. Eventually the fear of "being without" turned into the obsession "to have."

David cried out to God to be delivered from his unconscious faults and presumptuous sins. Let's review what the Word of God says:

> Who can discern his lapses and errors? Clear me from hidden [and unconscious] faults. Keep back Your servant also from presumptuous sins; let them not have dominion over me! Then shall I be blameless, and I shall be innocent and clear of great transgression.
>
> —PSALM 19:12–13, AMP

The great transgression is subliminal bondage. It makes a man fall when he *thinks* he is standing. The Bible says that we must be careful when we think we stand, lest we fall (1 Cor. 10:12)! There is a way that seems right to a man, but the end of it is death. We need to know when there is demonic presence in areas of our lives that are working against us undercover. I call it *undercover bondage*. The enemy comes to steal, kill and destroy. Destruction will run its course whether we recognize that it is there or not. Lord, help us to be open to the truth, and deliver us from our unconscious sins.

Demonic assignment

The strongman is the chief spirit that is assigned to garrison the stronghold. He reinforces the stronghold and ensures the victim's bondage through tight spiritual security. An example of a demonic assignment is the strongman of death, which comes to release the spirit of suicide. Death is the strongman, and suicide is the assignment. You can usually know the assignment by the presence of the strongman.

Another example is the strongman of Jezebel. By studying the characteristics of Jezebel (such as control, witchcraft, false prophecy) you can understand the assignment of the spirit. Often spirits will speak through the mouth of the person and reveal their assignment. A spirit may say, "I make her see things!" We would be safe to say that this was a strongman of divination operating; its assignment is to open up a third eye in her life.

Point of origination

Demons are stupid! Ninety percent of the time they tell on themselves. The only way you find out the true point of origination of a spirit is when it is revealed to you by the Holy Spirit or by one of the demons.

I would not suggest that anyone make it a habit to have conversations with demons. Demons are liars. They have no truth in them, but they can give you pertinent facts to a person's deliverance. The anointing will lock a devil up and make it talk!

On one occasion, we were ministering deliverance to the entire staff at a church that had been through a major church split. A key leader took half of the members and started a new ministry. This brought much turmoil in the midst of the congregation that was left. A few of the people who left later returned to the ministry to restore their fellowship. During the deliverance sessions all of the people that returned had the same manifestation. A demon, in the same voice as the leader who began the split, cried out of all of these people. This was a strong case of transference of spirits.

As the demon left the last person, it laughed, "I will just jump in someone else in the church!" This was the spirit of Azazel, the scapegoat demon. It was entering the hearts of the people through sympathetic magic. *Sympathetic magic* is an ungodly control through the spirit of sympathy.

We knew we needed to bind the "transfer of spirits," so we pleaded the blood over the congregation. It is important to get to the root of the problem so that old manifestations will not recur and spread like bad weeds.

Grasp the principle of binding and loosing

To operate effectively in deliverance ministry, the worker must grasp the principle of binding and loosing. As we learned earlier, the Greek word for *bind* is *deo,* and it means "to tie up like a dog; to forbid to operate." Binding restricts the activity of the enemy and renders him helpless through warfare prayer. Another Greek word is *deomai,* which means "to tie oneself to in prayer." This indicates intercessory confrontation, or to stand in the gap in the spirit. The Greek word for *loose* is *luo,* "to break up, destroy and dissolve." It literally means to cause to be seen no more. We are called to *destroy* the strongholds of the enemy and to make a path for the will of God to be released in the earth realm. We have been given the keys (*kleis*) to shut down and close up the work of the enemy. The gates of hell shall not prevail against the church.

The practice of sin and unbelief

The practice of sin and unbelief among deliverance workers will hinder the effectiveness of the ministry presented. The seven sons of Sceva were rejected by the demon spirits when they attempted to deliver a demon-possessed man (Acts 19:14–16). The sons of Sceva were vagabonds. They had no spiritual or physical connection. They were uncovered. The Bible also says they were exorcists. Deliverance workers must be distinguished from exorcists. An exorcist is not a true deliverance worker. An exorcist does not have a relationship with God. Many will stand rejected before God and say, "We have cast out devils in your name." They were exorcists, not true deliverance workers. They did not have a relationship with God.

Effective deliverance workers need:

- A legitimate covering by constituted apostolic authority
- A solid connection with team workers to back them up with intercession and prophetic support
- A clean heart and right spirit, which gives the ability to minister in compassion
- A lifestyle of holiness and discipline, which pleases God and would not bring Him to open shame

The focus should always be on the Lord.

It is very dangerous to draw attention to yourself. Jesus is the Deliverer, and He knows exactly what He is doing. Keeping your eyes on Jesus will help you not to be anxious. "Be anxious for nothing, but in everything by prayer and supplication, with thanksgiving, let your requests be made known to God" (Phil. 4:6).

Hebrews 12:2 says that we should continue to look unto Jesus, "the author and finisher of our faith." When you keep your eyes on Jesus, you will be delivered from childish games. All believers, including the youngest child or the newest Christian, have the power to cast out devils from their own lives. However, I must warn you that deliverance ministry is not a toy to pull out and play with just because you are bored. It is nothing to play with. Ephesians 5:1–4 teaches that we should follow God as children follow their daddy. Jesus said that we must approach the gospel as little children. The best deliverance workers are workers who forget all that they think they know and come to God as a child. Though we must be childlike in our learning, we also must be mature in our living. Verse 4 of the same passage states that we should not participate in foolish talking or jesting that is not convenient.

Confidentiality is of utmost importance!

During deliverance sessions demons sometimes manifest themselves in ways that are embarrassing to the person receiving ministry. Recently we were ministering deliverance to a young lady who did not appear to have any deep bondage. When I noticed spirits on the young lady's hands, I slapped her hands with my hand. The demons threw the young lady across the office with a strong force.

It caught myself and the other two team members off guard. We took a moment to get ourselves together, and then we began to call the spirits out by revelation from the Spirit of God. One of the team members called out a spirit of "false pregnancy." The demon threw the young lady on her back in the position of giving birth to a baby. She began to go into a demonic labor.

In thirteen years of deliverance ministry, I had never witnessed anything like that. The young lady was actually pushing with labor pains as if she were giving birth to a real child. I believe this was her first time of going through any kind of deliverance session. I do not know what gripped her worse—the fear or the embarrassment. As I looked into her face, her clothes were disheveled and her hair was a disaster. The compassion that we all felt for her that day was unexplainable. I hate the devil!

Familiar spirits often tell personal secrets that the person may not have wanted to disclose. There have even been cases when the person shares incidents of adultery, fornication or other past or present sins from which he or she desires to be delivered. To protect both the minister and the person receiving deliverance:

- The person receiving ministry should sign a "ministry release form" to release the person performing the ministry from any frivolous lawsuits.

- The minister(s) should be made to sign a "confidentiality form" acknowledging the importance of protecting the privacy rights of the person(s) receiving ministry.

Teamwork is the key.

Jesus never sent the disciples out alone. God does not have any "lone rangers" or "solo soldiers." I try to have at least three people on my team when doing private deliverance sessions. This team consists of:

- *A coach*—This individual leads the session and sets the pace for the session. He is dependent on the other two members to help him as they hear from the Lord. The coach should be the main person communicating with the individual receiving ministry to avoid three people speaking in different directions at one time. The other team members should keep their eyes on the coach for him/her to let them in and release them from leading the ministry at times (as the Lord leads).

- *An intercessor*—This individual stands in the gap through intercession and warfare throughout the session. The overall mission is to direct the spirits where to go when they come out and to cover everyone involved in prayer. The intercessor also listens for instructions from the Lord to give to the coach. The intercessor assures that prayer goes forth before, during and after the session (binding all backlash and retaliation and forbidding any spirits to follow anyone home).

- *Support personnel*—This individual provides buckets, towels, anointing oil or whatever is needed to support the session. This person is the armorbearer of the team, but must also support in prayer and discernment as the Lord chooses to use him or her.

Rid your home and heart of all idolatry.

At any cost, avoid the curse of Ai. (See Joshua 7.) Joshua lost this battle even though the Israelites were fighting against just a small group of people. It was not their ability to fight that made them lose the battle. They lost the battle because of "the accursed thing." This term relates to anything that has been dedicated unto destruction, or that which God has called you to separate from.

It is for this reason that a relationship with God is so important in deliverance ministry. Only God can confirm the accursed thing in your heart. Ministers can pray for your house to be emptied out, and they can advise you of the steps you need to take, but you must also have a revelation and release the object from your heart.

At the beginning of my ministry, I did not have an eye for fetishes. A *fetish* is a cursed object. A warfare preacher came to our church and changed our lives forever. He was a meticulous brain surgeon. He taught us warfare prayer, but he also taught me about fetishes. I received an impartation that week that changed my life. I have always been able to see in the spirit realm, but I could now see demons resting on objects. If a cursed object was a hundred miles away, I could spot it. We did a spiritual housecleaning in the church and in our homes. Since that time, our finances, the ministry and my family have been touched by unbelievable increase.

Team ministry is very important. The first time our teams ministered at a major conference was at the Congress on Deliverance in 1999. This conference is overseen by Peter and Doris Wagner of the World Prayer Center in Colorado Springs.

This conference was a type of pilot project that God placed on Dr. Wagner's heart.

The success of this conference should be recorded in the record books. Homeless people to millionaires were miraculously set free by the power of God. Teams participated from around the world. I believe the true success of this pioneering project was the resulting organizational structure, apostolic covering and overall willingness of the believers attending to let the Holy Ghost have His way. Every team did not operate in the same capacity or use the same approach, but all were effective.

I personally witnessed and experienced the truth of 1 Corinthians 12:4–7 coming to life in a powerful way.

> Now there are diversities of gifts, but the same Spirit. And there are differences of administrations, but the same Lord. And there are diversities of operation, but it is the same God which worketh all in all. But the manifestation of the Spirit is given to every man to profit withal.
>
> —KJV

It is important to consider the following words:

- *Differences* (diairesis)—This word means "to have distinction or character that recognizes a person or ministry in their uniqueness." It also means "to be set apart in the midst of a variety; concerning assigned gifts."

- *Operations* (energema)—This word means "to perform a function or assigned task." It means "to be active and effective in a gift."

- *Administrations* (diakonia)—This is a word that refers to the way a person serves, ministers or administers in their particular gift.

Based on the above definitions, the following is true in reference to how God uses us in our gifts:

- *Differences are who we are.*
- *Operations are what we do.*
- *Administrations are how we do it.*

THREE DELIVERANCE APPROACHES

Based on my observations at the Congress on Deliverance and the revelation that the Lord gave me concerning them, I learned about three deliverance approaches that were highlighted in my heart.

1. The counseling approach

This approach was effectively activated by Doris Wagner. Her approach simply gives the person receiving deliverance a checklist that he/she completes before the counseling session is started. Mrs. Wagner's approach requires that the deliverance ministers study and pray over the list and begin ministering by the information given (being led by the Holy Spirit during the duration of the sessions).

This is not the particular approach that we find effective in our administration of deliverance because of the heavy prophetic mantle on our team members. However, I've found it to be effective in Mrs. Wagner's ministry, as many are being set free through the administration of the gift of deliverance that God has given her.

2. The inner healing approach

This approach was effectively put into action by Peter Horrobin of Ellel Ministries. Ellel is an international network of deliverance and teaching centers that house students from around the world. Students are trained, activated and sent into the mission field. Dr Horrobin has a unique way of breaking bondages down methodically by teaching the Word of God. Though some counseling is included, it is not as in-depth as the counseling approach.

From my observations, this type of ministry brings a realization to the person receiving deliverance as to the actual root of the problem and opens that person up to being delivered from it. This approach entails renunciation of what the person is being delivered from and confession of what they are to walk in afterwards. Many ministers who operate in deliverance ministry do not support inner healing. It is merely another form of deliverance, and as long as we are not psychoanalyzing demons, I am all for it.

3. The confrontational approach

This approach is the approach that God uses with most of the demon busters at Spoken Word. We use all three kinds of approaches mentioned in this chapter at our home church, but evangelistically we walk in the confrontational approach. The nickname for our deliverance team is *the Dirty Dozen*. It is just a fun way that we do God's business.

We are sometimes criticized for our unusual way of administration, but we get more support than complaints. *(Ain't nobody mad but the devil.)* Deliverance is hard work, and it should be fun. Because of the time that we spend doing it, we need to enjoy it when we do it. The confrontational approach is when we simply address the forces of hell head-on. This approach takes a high level of dedication and discipline. People who participate on teams that use the confrontational deliverance approach must be bold, prophetic and totally submitted to the apostolic.

The warfare is great in all three approaches, but I must say that the warfare in the confrontational approach is the epitome of them all. The Bible says that the weapons of our warfare are not carnal, but mighty through God to the pulling down of strongholds (2 Cor. 10:4).

The word we need to highlight in this passage is *warfare*. This word is *strateia* in the Greek, and it means "apostolic career of hardship." The warfare in confrontational deliverance is great. But we take comfort in the fact that "where sin abounded, grace abounded much more" (Rom. 5:20). We have seen great warfare as we go in to get captives and bring them out. But on the other hand, we have seen greater moves of God than the warfare that the enemy has sent against us. The greater one is on the inside of us! There is no wrong or right. A deliverance team must plug into the overall vision of its covering and allow the Lord to use it in each team member's anointing. There are many approaches to deliverance team ministry. Though I address our approach as the confrontational approach, I like the phrase "Dirty Dozen Approach." (In the following paragraphs I will describe this approach more thoroughly.) *The Dirty Dozen* was a movie about a group of low-down men from terrible backgrounds who were called on to go behind enemy lines and recover soldiers who had been taken captive. They were selected from death row in prison. Their mission was considered a suicide mission, and they were not considered a great loss. They were not expected to come out of the mission alive. The dirty dozen had nothing to lose.

This sounds like Revelation 12:11: "And they did not love their lives to the death." My first deliverance team consisted of ex-prostitutes, former drug addicts, former witches and ex-alcoholics. We had nothing to lose! If we did not cast the devil out, he would cast us out and send us back to spiritual prison. Most people in confrontational deliverance ministry are not there by choice. Because of the confrontational circumstances out of which they have come, they are forced to confront the demonic nose to nose. "The kingdom of heaven suffers violence, and the violent take it by force" (Matt. 11:12)!

On page 150 I have included a chart showing the biblical names for the devil and the references where these names may be found. This chart will be helpful to you as you prepare to do deliverance ministry. The more you know about the enemy and his tactics, the better prepared you will be to do battle in a deliverance ministry.

BIBLICAL NAMES FOR THE DEVIL

Biblical Name	Root/Meaning	Reference
Abaddon	Hebrew: Destroyer	Revelation 9:11
Accuser of the brethren		Revelation 12:10
Adversary	One who stands against	1 Peter 5:8
Angel of the bottomless pit		Revelation 9:11
Antichrist	The one against Christ	1 John 4:3
Apollyon	Greek: Destroyer	Revelation 9:11
Beelzebub	God of the flies, dung god	Matthew 12:24; Mark 3:22; Luke 11:15
Belial		2 Corinthians 6:15
Devil	False accuser, devil, slanderer	Matthew 4:1; Luke 4:2, 6; Revelation 20:2
Enemy		Matthew 13:39
Evil spirit		1 Samuel 16:14
Father of all liars		John 8:44
God of this world		2 Corinthians 4:4
Great red dragon		Revelation 12:3
Lucifer	Son of the morning (star)	Isaiah 14:12
Man of sin		2 Thessalonians 2:3
Murderer		John 8:44
Old serpent		Revelation 12:9; 20:2
Power of darkness		Colossians 1:13
Prince of this world		John 12:31; 14:30; 16:11
Prince of the power of the air		Ephesians 2:2
Ruler of darkness		Ephesians 6:12
Satan	Hebrew: Adversary Greek: Accuser	1 Chronicles 21:1; Job 1:6; John 13:27; Acts 5:3; 26:18; Romans 16:20
Serpent		Genesis 3:4, 14; 2 Corinthians 11:3
Son of perdition	Destruction, ruin, waste, loss	John 17:12
Tempter		Matthew 4:3; 1 Thessalonians 3:5
Thief		John 10:10
Wicked one		Matthew 13:19, 38

THE DIRTY DOZEN
DELIVERANCE APPROACH

I personally admire the different types of deliverance approaches as long as they are effective in setting the captives free. I may drive one route from Jacksonville, Florida, to Atlanta, Georgia, and another person may take another route. As long as we reach our destination, we have all served our purpose.

I would like to share the details of our particular deliverance approach and share a few case studies. It is my prayer that this information will bless you.

Our ministry teams consist of three members:

- *Coach*—team leader
- *Intercessor*—prays before, after and during deliverance
- *Support*—aids team in any way possible

The deliverance teams operate as follows:

Identifying the spirits

All team members are intercessors and are trained to know the different types of spirits. Each team member is trained to identify many strongmen and different spirits. Spirits we have not studied are sometimes revealed in sessions.

Our successes

We have experienced much success in one-session deliverances. I have often witnessed this kind of anointing on the evangelistic field. However, there have been times when I have personally walked homosexuals, ex-witches and drug addicts through sessions that took place over a couple of years. Most of the follow-up sessions include recovery care, whereby we minister to the brokenhearted and wounded in spirit.

Whenever there appears to be more demonic infiltration in follow-up sessions than encountered in the first session, we attempt to find out where and how the Baal-peor (lord of the opening) is operating, and we close the door. Most of the time doors are opened through a lack of spiritual discipline, negative habits or a contaminated work or home environment. We do have forms available for people who have been delivered, helping them to recognize things that may cause doors to the demonic to open back up in their lives.

Confidentiality

Most of our deliverance sessions are done in private rooms that have been set apart for the occasion. There have been times demons have manifested, and we were not afforded the opportunity of immediate privacy. If we detect that a spirit will do embarrassing things to a person, we prayerfully move them to a private area. This movement must be Spirit-led or it can be detrimental to the person's deliverance. I believe demons manifest for a few reasons:

- To put on a show or to embarrass the person. (Even though satan's power is in deception, demons sometimes like attention.)

- The spirit is at a weak point, and the anointing has caused it manifest. At this point the demon is gullible and ready to be cast out. Sometimes in moving a person out of the will of God, we can miss the moment and quench the anointing. This is why spiritual discernment (not just the discerning of spirits but discerning also how to move in the spirit) is of utmost importance.

Often (not all the time) during sessions people will release body fluids. This is one of the manifestations of demons exiting a body. Body fluid excretion is not always a manifestation of deliverance. Over the past nine years of deliverance ministry, I have noticed some of the following body fluid excretion manifestations:

- When Caribbean voodoo is involved, the person

usually has mucus draining from the nose and may even make hissing noises by blowing through their noses.

- Coughing and a profuse release of saliva are usual occurrences.

- When witchcraft is involved (either by "use" or "contact"), mucus mixed with blood can come from the mouth or nose.

- A few times (very rarely) we have experienced a person wetting his or her clothes when a spirit left the body. Others have an extreme urgency to go to the restroom.

Because of the above possibilities, we keep paper towels, buckets and throw covers available.

The deliverance session

The deliverance sessions we have encountered range from dealing with unforgiveness to a person who was possessed by the spirit of eidolon and python, which is one of the most deadly combinations of divination spirits to encounter. The manifestations in our deliverance sessions range from tears to physical transformations. We have no way of foreseeing how long a deliverance session will last. Our sessions have ranged from ten minutes to three hours (and sometimes longer).

We follow these guidelines:

1. Make sure the area is consecrated.

2. Everyone involved comes into agreement. (In cases where family members or friends bring people in that are under the influence to the point of incapacitation, we pray over the person and break the power of the ruler spirit over their head.)

3. Intercession is then made to discern *if* it is time to go forth in deliverance. If the Spirit of God does not lead

us to do deliverance at the time presented, we pray a hedge of protection around the person to keep him or her in a safe place until the time of deliverance.

4. Intercession is done for revelation and discerning of spirits. We were ministering to a twenty-three-year-old lady one time when I had a vision of the young lady curled up in the corner of an attic as a little girl. The Spirit revealed that she was physically abused at ten years of age, and demonic infiltration had taken place. The spirits involved were rejection, unforgiveness, abuse, resentment and torment.

Revelation of other occurrences in her life led us to the strongman whose name was *Raja* (a nymphomaniac spirit). Raja spoke through the young lady in a demonic voice, further revealing itself to us. After research we found more information on this spirit.

When dealing with demons that are speaking through people, discernment must be sharp enough to recognize if the demon is lying or not. We are very careful not to allow spirits to have monologues. This also takes discernment. You must know when to bind the spirits and when to let them speak. The devil often tells on himself. Spirits began to speak through a young lady being delivered from witchcraft and homosexuality. The spirit said, "She is mine; she was dedicated at birth, and we have thirty days to kill her." This information gave us the keys to unlock the strongman's hold.

5. Once the spirits are revealed, we call them out in the name of Jesus. While the spirits are exiting the person, an intercessor is available to direct them where to go. The intercessor also covers everyone involved in the deliverance session.

If proper precautions are not taken, spirits that have been cast out will linger in the place where the deliverance was held or will follow the minister home. The demons can also enter innocent bystanders or those not covered by the blood of Jesus or who are territorially out of place. It is very dangerous for people living in sin to cast out demons. Territorial spirits can enter this person if he or she is operating in a realm outside the covering on that person's life. This prompts us to know the lifestyles of our team members.

Before, during and after ministry, intercession is a must. Certain spirits can only be dealt with after a period of fasting and prayer. It is not always proper to attack deliverance cases immediately based on circumstances. Some cases require seeking the face of God on how to approach them. I have found that some witches come to churches to seek deliverance only for the reward of getting seven times the demons for more power. A consistent prayer life with spiritual discernment is a must.

RECENT CASE STUDIES

I am including the following case studies to help you see how we have used this "Dirty Dozen" approach in our own deliverance ministry.

A businessman

Case background—I received a call from a young lady with whom I had a very successful deliverance session. She shared with a business friend how she had received deliverance from a spirit of python through my ministry. He showed a slight interest in meeting with me because he felt that this spirit might be hindering the finances in his business.

The next day he called her, urgently requesting to meet with me, and we set an appointment. The middle-aged man had been saved for approximately five years and was knowledgeable of the spirit realm. At one time he had been addicted to drugs, and he now helps people who are indigent or in bondage to drugs. His business had been dedicated to God for the past few years, but a couple of lesbians who were involved in the occult used to work there. These two women had a great effect on the receptionist, who was eventually fired. They had persuaded her to sue the company. All three of these women left bitter and spoke curses against the office.

Session: I was the coach on this team, and I had two people assisting me. We started the session by letting the businessman express himself concerning what he was experiencing. He explained that he had been through levels of deliverance from a deliverance ministry very well known throughout the nation. He shared that curses had been verbally broken and that he had renounced many things from his past.

Next, we began to pray. We came in agreement and welcomed the Holy Spirit in to lead us. The Lord led us to pray as we walked throughout his office. There were a few cursed items in the place, but generally the place was free from fetishism. Then the Lord gave me a vision of the building with an unusually dark, black snake curled around it. The tail of the snake was sticking straight up in the air. As I came to a particular place in the building, the Holy Spirit said, "Hot spot."

When I shared this with the businessman, he said the two lesbians would meet in this area and smoke cigarettes. This is where the snake tail stuck up. We commanded the spirit to leave as we stood at the point of the "hot spot." We consecrated the grounds and initiated deliverance to the businessman. On immediate command the demons began to come out. Mucus flowed profusely from his mouth, and we could feel the demons moving around in his belly. He had to renounce some things, which brought on a great breakthrough.

Results—The root of his bondage was "neglecting to deal with issues" as far back as his childhood. He was holding a lot of things inside and operating in a false peace. Once the realization of this took place, the demons that were holding on to these cords had nothing left to hold on to. The drug addiction and other bondages were only symptoms of the root problem. He had been given other medications to deal with anxiety and other conditions diagnosed in psychological analysis, which only made matters worse. The cocaine and prescription drugs had opened the door for the spirit of pharmekeia (medication by magic) to come in. The spirit of Pan (fear and panic) was also causing restlessness and anxiety. The businessman was very weak after the session, but he said he felt as if weights had been lifted off his shoulders.

A nursing health aide

Case background—A woman spoke to me before one service to inform me that her daughter's aunt, who was a Christian, was being attacked by an Incubus spirit. The attacks were occurring more often, and she was afraid to go to sleep. I made an appointment to see the young lady after service that day. During the service, a spirit of religion manifested and began to throw the young lady around the room as she screamed very loudly. We had her taken downstairs.

There was a room in the basement of the church we called the "yes" room. As we took people down the stairs, they would often begin to shake their head and say "no" under demonic influence. This was the case with this young lady. The demons were manifesting from the service, so we immediately felt led to begin deliverance.

Session: The young lady began to growl. I was the support person and one of my pastors was the coach. I knew that there was some type of beast spirit present, but I could not put my finger on it. The Holy Spirit revealed to me there was a "dog" spirit in her. When I called out what I heard in the spirit, the young lady's hands and feet began to physically turn under like an animal. She then sat up like a dog on two feet, with her hands in a paw-like position, and began to pant like a dog. Her body began to make sexual gestures like a dog having sex. This body gesture was so intense and violent that she passed out on the floor.

Because of the seriousness of the nature of her bondage, I called my husband in to help. Up to this point, the session consisted of calling out spirits as the Holy Spirit revealed them. Very little mucus was released from this young lady during her deliverance, but she passed gases from her body as the demons came out. The main manifestations were violent body jerking and foul odor. The spirits talked through her and screamed violently as they exited.

Results—This session took three to four hours, but the young lady was released from the bondage of the spirits. We found out after the session that this young lady was a health aide nurse, and she was assigned to sit for a warlock who practiced spirit travel. He would attack her as she fell asleep while she was sitting with him. She shared with me that a few days before we ministered deliverance to her, she had fallen asleep at work. From her description of the incident, it is apparent that a nightmare spirit attacked her. She was unable to move, but a dog came up behind her and had intercourse with her. This is how the dog spirit entered. We had not known this in the natural, but the Holy Spirit revealed it with her confirmation.

We received another confirmation when the spirit came out, for it manifested like a dog. The young lady's face looked totally different after the session, and as far as we know, the Incubus spirit ceased to visit her in her sleep. She did have to change her place of employment.

Chapter 11

Supernatural Protection in Deliverance Ministry

PSALM 91 IS filled with God's promises for His people. In this psalm, God is addressed in four ways that show His love for us. This poetic scripture provides a specific description of how God cares for us. It is a promise that He will protect and preserve us through all dangers, at all times and in all circumstances. In this psalm, God is called:

- The Most High—verses 1, 9
- The Almighty (*Shaddai*)—verse 1
- The Lord (*Yahweh*)—verses 2, 9
- My God—verse 2

There is a place in God where our enemies are rendered inoperative. David speaks in terms of dwelling and abiding with God. The word *dwelling* is the Hebrew word *yashab*, meaning "to have one's abode." This abode is a continuous state of like-mindedness with Christ. The word *abide* is the Hebrew word *lun*, meaning "to lodge or pass the night." David tells us to dwell in the *secret place*, or *cether*, under the covering, shelter or shade of *El Shaddai*. This is a place of intimacy, which requires discipline yet provides security from demonic infiltration.

Deliverance team ministers must live close to God.

> Be well balanced (temperate, sober of mind), be vigilant
> and cautious at all times; for that enemy of yours, the
> devil, roams around like a lion roaring [in fierce hunger],
> seeking someone to seize upon and devour.
>
> —1 PETER 5:8, AMP

We must stay close to God, for in His vicinity there is great safety. Psalm 91:2 declares that the Lord is our refuge and fortress, *Elohim*, who is our ruler and judge, on whom we will rely and confidently trust. When you allow God to be your refuge, you will not be snatched from or plucked out of His hands by the trapper or bait-layer. Who is the trapper or bait-layer? It is the one who comes to kill, steal and destroy.

No weapon formed against you will prosper if you make the Lord your place of habitation. You will have God's covering. It is His truth and His faithfulness that become your "shield and buckler" (v. 4). The word *shield* is the Hebrew word *tsinnah*, which means "something piercing."

With God's protection, you won't have to fear the terror of night—the heliophobic demons (demons who come out at night to terrorize), subterranean demons (demons who live in caves like trolls), aqueous demons (demons who live in water, even drinking water) or aerial demons (demons who hover around). You don't have to fear Abaddon or Apollyon (the destroyer), the demon of death, Beelzebub (lord of the flies) or Molech (untimely death). Satan's ground troops (terrestrial demons who inhabit forests and fields) are inoperative as well. But the Word of the Lord is operative, working for you.

There are certain guarantees that we have:

- Protection from attack
- No fear of destruction
- The ministry of guardian angels
- Deliverance that lasts

David lets us know that these spirits may fall at our side, but they can't approach us. "A thousand may fall at your side, and ten thousand at your right hand; but it shall not come near you" (v. 7).

Neither Incubus nor Succubus can invade your body and have intercourse with you. David calls you a *spectator* to demonic attack because of the devil's inability to reach you in the secret place of the Most High. No evil, plague or calamity will befall or come near you (v. 10).

Do you understand the implication of this? A way of escape has already been made. You just have to get in God!

Further, we have the ministry of guardian angels over us. They will accompany you, defend you and preserve you as you obey and serve God. They will bear you up before you fall (vv. 11–12). Through the angels, who are commissioned by God, you have divine protection.

Then, notice the authority you have as attested to by verse 13. This verse sounds like Luke 10:19: "Behold, I give you the authority to trample on serpents and scorpions, and over all the power of the enemy, and nothing shall by any means hurt you." The lion and the adder, the young lion and the serpent shall be under your feet. God has publicly committed to "heal the broken-hearted, to proclaim liberty to the captives, and the opening of the prison to those who are bound" (Isa. 61:1). The devil is only committed to our shame. We need to bring him to an open shame.

How do you get to this place of guaranteed complete deliverance? The only way is by loving and knowing God. You have a promise to be set securely on high (seated in high places with Christ Jesus) because of an intimate relationship, which excludes any syncretism with darkness. This is a promise of deliverance. *Deliverance* is the Hebrew word *pallet*, which means "to escape, to slip away or to bring into security."

Does this mean you will never be attacked? No. But this is your escape when you are attacked. Here's the formula:

- You set your love on Him.
- You have a personal knowledge of His mercy, love and kindness.
- You trust and rely on Him and know that He will never forsake you.
- When you are under attack, guess what? You just call on Him.
- He answers, gives you extra protection, delivers you and honors you.
- Then you will have long life and the promise of eternal life with the Father.

TRANSFERENCE OF SPIRITS

One of the greatest fears that people have in dealing with deliverance issues is the fear that they will pick up spirits while ministering or being ministered to. Transference of spirits is a reality, but when we obey the Word of God when dealing with unclean spirits, we will not be contaminated. Azazel is the spirit that we have identified as the strongman of "transference of spirits." This spirit is called a "desert spirit" or "scapegoat spirit" in most occult dictionaries. (I do not recommend that people dabble into occult dictionaries without the leading of the Holy Spirit; there are saints that specialize in this area who can get the information and release it in God's timing and Spirit.)

Denzel Washington played a role in a popular movie *Fallen*, in which demons were transferring to people by physical contact. The name of the spirit in the movie was *Azazel*. The Lord prompted me to research this name. I found this name in an occult dictionary, but to my surprise it was also in the *American Heritage Dictionary* and even in *Webster's Dictionary*.

This name is defined as the evil spirit in the wilderness to whom a scapegoat was sent on the Day of Atonement. The name literally means "removal from one to another." In the movie *Fallen*, this spirit (Azazel) jumped from one person to another.

The slightest contact with this spirit caused the countenances of people to change.

In a natural sense a scapegoat is "one that was made to bear the blame of others." In the Bible a scapegoat was the live goat over whose head Aaron confessed all the sins of the children of Israel on the Day of Atonement. This scapegoat was sent into the wilderness. The *American Heritage Dictionary* leads us to believe that the scapegoat was sent to a spirit called "Azazel" in the wilderness. I did not pay much attention to this until I heard demons (calling themselves Azazel) manifesting in people to whom I ministered deliverance. To my further amazement, I found the demon Azazel in the Bible. Let's review the scripture together:

> He shall take the two goats and present them before the Lord at the door of the Tent of Meeting. Aaron shall cast lots on the two goats—one lot for the Lord, the other lot for *Azazel* or removal. And Aaron shall bring the goat on which the Lord's lot fell and offer him as a sin offering. But the goat on which the lot fell for *Azazel* or removal shall be presented alive before the Lord to make atonement over him, that he may be let go in the wilderness for *Azazel* (for dismissal).
>
> —LEVITICUS 16:7–10, AMP, EMPHASIS ADDED

This scripture tells us that the sins were sent into the wilderness for Azazel (the scapegoat). The sins of the people were transferred to Azazel. These sins represented that which was demonic in the lives of the people. Can we be safe to say that sin is demonic? Sin never dies, but it creates death. James said lust is conceived, sin is birthed and when it is fully grown, death is achieved (James 1:15).

The path of sin is:

- *Conception*—the seed of the act in the person's life
- *Birth*—the act in a person's life
- *Achievement*—the goal of the act in a person's life

The purpose of the atonement was to reconcile man unto

God, but another meaning for atonement is "to make obsolete." What was made obsolete? We must understand that there is no reconciliation unto God unless the sins (demons) are removed. I think it would help a lot of people if they would see sin in direct relationship with demons. There is no power in making up pretty names for sins to make people feel better about it. It is time to call a spade a spade!

We often struggle with deliverance terminology such as "possession." Some walk on eggshells in using this term in reference to Christians. I choose not to play the game. It is popular, but there is no power in it. God is not impressed! *To possess* means to "occupy," and if demons occupy a territory in our lives, they possess it.

This is a hard word, but the truth is that a Christian who cannot stop using cocaine is out of control. The enemy is occupying an area of that person's life, and that person possesses no control. Where we do not possess control, the devil will possess control. The key word is not just occupancy but "control." I can possess what I can control.

The reason Jesus wants us to occupy is because He wants us to "control" (in His stead). A majority in *presence* does not necessarily indicate a majority in *power*. There are many countries with thousands of poor people who have no power over their circumstances.

My point is that we are not just to be present in the earth realm. We must show up and show out! We must be "present in power"! One Christian believer can put a thousand demons to flight, and two believers can put ten thousand to flight. On the other hand, if you connect with a Christian who does not believe, you would be better off alone. It is not the *presence* of a Christian that shakes hell; it is the *power* of a believer! The purpose of demonic infiltration in the life of a believer is to make him or her live a life of doubt. People with heavy demonic activity in their lives have a hard time believing God. The devil knows that without faith it is impossible to please God. Without faith we are "damned."

In Mark 16, Jesus appeared to the eleven:

> Later He appeared to the eleven as they sat at the table; and He rebuked their unbelief and hardness of heart, because they did not believe those who had seen Him after He had risen. And He said to them, "Go into all the world and preach the gospel to every creature. He who believes and is baptized will be saved; but he who does not believe will be condemned [damned, KJV]. And these signs will follow those who believe: In My name they will cast out demons; they will speak with new tongues; they will take up serpents; and if they drink anything deadly, it will by no means hurt them; they will lay hands on the sick, and they will recover."
> —MARK 16:14–18

I take a radical position toward this scripture because it clearly references some serious issues about believers. My interpretation of this message is that this scripture refers to more than accepting Jesus in our hearts as Savior. The eleven disciples were already Christians, but the scripture says that they had unbelief and hardness of heart. Their problem was that they did not believe the reports from those who had seen Jesus *after* He had risen.

I believe that this is a spirit released against the body of Christ. We know Jesus on the cross, but there is a problem with knowing Him *after the Resurrection.* The power of the cross comes *after the cross.* Religion will keep Jesus on the cross!

I don't know about you, but *I have to have the power!* When we know Him through His resurrection power (in us), we can have a heyday against the demonic. This scripture says that those who believe not shall be "damned." The word flows with precision into the revelation of what Jesus was talking about. Can I paraphrase it? He told them, "Just in case you do not know what I mean when I am talking about believing Me…I will give you the signs that will follow them who *really* believe Me." Do I have to go any further? You know what I'm talking about!

- Casting out devils
- Speaking in tongues
- Taking up serpents
- Laying hands on the sick

I'm talking about Resurrection power! Hallelujah! This is what being a believer is all about—having power over the devil and his crew. But our real rejoicing rests in the fact that our names are written in the Lamb's Book of Life!

The word *damned* may seem harsh, but the gospel is not a tip-toe-through-the-tulips kind of Word. It is tight, but it's right! The word *damned* in the Greek is *katakrino*, and it means "to be *judged, sentenced* and *condemned*." If you take a serious look at what Jesus was saying, you will not get offended. If you do not believe in the ministries listed above, then you judge, sentence and condemn yourself.

Religion wants us to limit this passage to salvation, but I believe it encompasses far more than that. I choose to take the radical position rather than the easy way out. If we do not cast out devils, we abide with them. If we do not believe in healing, we die. If we do not take up serpents, they will take us up.

The Word tells us that if we drink any deadly thing, it will not harm us. This is a word of relief! This scripture assures us that if we run into a demon that can contaminate our body unto death, we can walk out of that encounter whole. God promises us protection from transference of spirits in warfare. This kind of confrontation takes faith. This is a faith that believes past Jesus dying for our sins. This faith takes us into the realm of belief that Jesus not only died for our sins, but He was also raised from the dead in Resurrection power.

The kicker is that the same power that raised Him from the dead is on the inside of you! You have to make this thing personal and take it for yourself. The same power that raised Jesus from the dead is not only in Benny Hinn; it is a power made available to the End-Time believer. If we neglect that which Jesus left for us to protect us, we will commit spiritual suicide. It was a while before I discerned the fact that Mark 16:17 is a protection scripture. Psalm 91 gives us a revelation on how God protects us. Mark 16:17 gives us a revelation of how God has given us the authority (by His Spirit in us) to protect ourselves from the powers of darkness. God is our defense and the rock of our refuge (Ps. 94:22). But we must never forget that He has given us an offense in the spirit. We are not called to sit around waiting for the devil to bother us and living our lives by calling out to God to get him off us!

God said that we would be a "stick" in His hand and a "battle-ax" against the enemy. (See Ezekiel 37:19; Jeremiah 51:20.) God takes pleasure in seeing His children "wup" up on the devil's head. He has given us the keys to put devils in lock down. He promises us that they shall not prevail.

The greatest protection we have is the blood of Jesus! There is power in the blood. Under the covering of the blood, we have a supernatural release of power (from God) that designates us to walk in the ability to deal with demonic forces and come out whole. When we encounter the enemy, we do not have to fear him. He cannot cross the bloodline; only we can! When we are presenting our bodies a living sacrifice, holy unto God, the devil cannot infiltrate our temples! When we serve God halfheartedly and live double lives, we open the doors to the demonic. We cannot cast out what we are a part of.

Jesus had authority over the devil because the devil had no part in Him. When the devil has no part in us, we have authority over him. This is why he wants us to rent him a room in our lives. The Bible tells us to give no room to the devil (Eph. 4:27). To give him *room* in the Greek means to give him "license" or authoriza-tion. Where there is no license, the devil cannot operate. Not only does he need permission from God, but he also needs permission from us. If we do not give the devil a permit, he cannot build his kingdom in our lives. Remember that he has to have a permit to

build! We are called to tear his kingdom down; he is not supposed to build his kingdom in our lives.

BACK TO THE SPIRIT OF AZAZEL

It was pertinent that I explained the authority that we have over
the enemy before I addressed the issue of transference of spirits.
We must know that in our coast the enemy has no way to pene-
trate what is ours. God told Joshua that no man would be able
to stand before him as long as he was in his coast (Josh. 1:4–5).

The seven sons of Sceva were out of their coast, and the spirits
they attacked taught them a lesson. The Bible says that they took
it upon themselves to cast out devils. In deliverance, it is a very
important rule of thumb never to take on battles that you are
not called to fight. The Sceva brothers came in the name of Jesus
whom Paul preached. You must know and preach the gospel to
be effective in deliverance ministry. The Sceva brothers did not
know the Word, but they wanted to make a scene by casting out
devils when, in fact, the devils put them to open shame. The
spirit of shame was transferred to them because they were
unprepared for ministry.

There is so much we do not know about deliverance. We are
learning more every day. And I must make this statement on the
behalf of deliverance ministers everywhere: We are not *exorcists!*
My spirit is grieved when people refer to deliverance as an exorcism. The Word of the Lord tells us that this is error.

The seven sons of Sceva were exorcists; demons do not recognize exorcists. The demons declared, "Jesus I know, and Paul I
know; but who are you?" (Acts 19:15). Verse 13 tells us that Sceva
and his sons were vagabond Jews. The Bible refers to them as
exorcists. It also says they took upon themselves to cast out demons
by the Jesus whom Paul preached. The results were that the
demons in the man leaped on them, and they left the house naked.

A vagabond moves from place to place and has no physical or
spiritual roots. He is unsettled and irresponsible, and has a

disreputable and questionable lifestyle. Deliverance ministers must be settled spiritually and physically. They must lead lifestyles that are not a reproach among people lest they bring shame to the ministry of Jesus Christ. Last but not least, they must be rooted in deliverance to the point of living a well-balanced life with submission to a covering of apostolic authority.

Studying the biblical story on the Sceva family leads to me note the following:

1. There is a difference between exorcism and true deliverance.

2. A requirement for deliverance ministry is having a direct relationship with the Lord.

3. There must be the calling of God on an individual's life to do certain levels of deliverance ministry. People cannot take it upon themselves to jump into this ministry. (The seven sons of Sceva "took it upon themselves to call the name of the Lord Jesus over those who had evil spirits" [Acts 19:13].)

4. Demons do not recognize exorcists; they are only subject to those under an apostolic mandate.

5. The ministry of casting out devils must be accompanied with sound preaching of the gospel of Jesus Christ. The seven sons of Sceva did not preach Jesus, but they wanted to cast out devils.

Deliverance ministry is more than casting out devils. There will be some people who stand before God saying, "Lord, have we not cast out devils in Your name?" Witches and others who are rejected by God can cast out devils. They can command a devil to leave a person, because witches can operate by controlling spirits. A controlling spirit uses demons to control people, places and things. The notion that satan cannot cast out satan actually means that true deliverance cannot take place by demonic control. A witch can command a demon to leave a person temporarily, or they can move a spirit to another part of the person's body.

Deliverance ministry ministers to the whole man. Demonic oppression traumatizes a person, and these individuals need more than the devil cast out of them. The same spirits that are cast out of a person are seeking dry places. They are seeking bodies that have been swept clean and garnished. These spirits must have a body to fulfill their mission. It is torment to a devil to wander or have no place to abide. The Bible says we should give no room to the devil. We give him room when the rivers of living waters are not flowing in our lives. When there is no Word, there is no water.

"Out of his belly shall flow rivers of living water" (John 7:38). This represents the Holy Spirit of God. Without the Spirit, the Word and the light of God in our lives, we are open to demonic infiltration. The true anointing of deliverance ministry is not just to bring the people out of Egypt and leave them in the wilderness. The power of deliverance ministry is to take the people into the promised land. I believe God is raising up a generation that has the grace to lead His people into the promised land.

Some ministers would say that the things that occur in deliverance ministry are too radical and that it does not take all of that. Many say they do not believe in it. But those who say that could not have traveled with Jesus. Jesus said that if you are not with Him in this ministry, you are not with Him at all (Matt. 12:30). This is where the line is drawn in ministry. Everyone is not called to spearhead deliverance ministry, but every believer is called to cast out devils. Even if a leader does not feel the call of God to tap into the depths of this realm, he or she should provide an avenue for the people who desire to be delivered. Just as we have every kind of auxiliary you can name under the sun, every church needs a "devil-bustin' auxiliary."

Maybe that name is too radical for your church. Maybe you can call it an "inner-healing auxiliary." (Just do it, and call it something.) The church must provide a mechanism to help people get set free. Whenever Jesus came on the scene, the devils were provoked. The spirits that hid in the temple all the time came out of hiding when the anointing showed up. If you are truly anointed, it will provoke devils, and you need to know how to deal with them.

Why am I going into such depth concerning the sons of Sceva and the difference in exorcism and true deliverance? An exorcist is not protected from transference of spirits. In the movie *The Exorcist*, the demons jumped in the priest and made him commit suicide. This is biblical! This was the same thing that happened to the seven sons of Sceva.

When we cast out devils without the ministry of Jesus Christ (and this is possible), we are open to being beaten down by demons. The Bible warns us that there will be many who will say that they have cast out devils in Jesus' name (Matt. 7:22). They may have used His name illegitimately, but they avoided His ministry. The ministry of Jesus Christ has compassion for the soul of a man. This ministry does not just give the person immediate relief from the torment of devils; it ministers to "the whole man."

This is not a "boom, bam, thank you, ma'am" ministry. This is a "free indeed ministry." This is a ministry unto eternity, which is not just preparing us to make it through this life but the life to come. Those who are called to this ministry must be able to stand before God and hear the words, "Well done, my faithful servant."

To hear "I tell you I do not know you...Depart from Me, all you workers of iniquity" is what we should all fear (Luke 13:27). The worker of iniquity is not what the devil would want us to think it is. The worker of iniquity is not a street robber, prostitute or drug dealer. The word *iniquity* means one who has not accomplished the will of God while he was in the earth realm. The will of God is deeper than doing just *what God wants us to do*. We must perform His will *in the way God wants us to do it*.

When we do things our way, we open ourselves up to demonic spirits. This is what I call *territorial warfare*. It simply means operating in the realm of who, what, where, when and how God has called us to operate. God did not recognize those who had done things that would seem to please Him, the ones who stood before God in ultimate shame said, "We have cast out devils in your name." This would seem like such a great thing. Apparently God was not impressed. We often attempt to impress men, but it is important that we impress God. He recognizes only that which is in *His will.*

Jesus Himself said, "I have come down from heaven, not to do My own will, but the will of Him who sent Me" (John 6:38). We pick up extra baggage that weighs us down in the spirit when we do "our own thing." Rebellion and disobedience are two of the main door openers to transference of spirits.

Spirits transfer in three basic ways:

- Spirits transfer from person to person (Azazel).
- Spirits transfer from objects to persons (accursed thing).
- Spirits transfer from places to persons (territorial spirits).

The definition of the word *transfer* is "to convey or cause to pass from one *person, place* or *thing* to another."

ACCURSED THING

In the Book of Joshua, the spirit of death was transferred to Achan and his family when he partook of the accursed thing. (See Joshua 7.) We must note that the things that we partake of do not just affect us, but they also affect our bloodline. Apparently there was something that had attached itself to Achan and all that he owned. God commanded that it all be burned.

> Now Joshua said to Achan, "My son, I beg you, give glory to the LORD God of Israel, and make confession to Him, and tell me now what you have done; do not hide it from me." And Achan answered Joshua and said, "Indeed I have sinned against the LORD God of Israel, and this is what I

have done: When I saw among the spoils a beautiful Babylonian garment, two hundred shekels of silver, and a wedge of gold weighing fifty shekels, I coveted them and took them. And there they are, hidden in the earth in the midst of my tent, with the silver under it."...

Then Joshua, and all Israel with him, took Achan the son of Zerah, the silver, the garment, the wedge of gold, his sons, his daughters, his oxen, his donkeys, his sheep, his tent, and all that he had, and they brought them to the Valley of Achor. And Joshua said, "Why have you troubled us? The LORD will trouble you this day." So all Israel stoned him with stones; and they burned them with fire after they had stoned them with stones.

—JOSHUA 7:19–21, 24–25

Here are some important points to remember:

1. The camp had trouble because of the sin in one family.
2. The root spirit was covetousness (Achan desired things over what God had told him—idolatry).
3. Achan confessed but was still removed from the camp and executed.
4. We know that the lust for money is the root of all evil, but things can take a demonic place in our lives. We must pray about the things we allow into our homes. The Babylonian garment was a fetish (an object with demons attached to it).

TERRITORIAL SPIRITS

The man from Judah suffered from the transference of a territorial spirit when he did not go the way that God told him to go. God's instructions to him were, "You shall not eat bread, nor drink water, nor return by the same way you came" (1 Kings 13:9). When he went in the direction that God had warned him not to go, spirits of failure and death were transferred to him.

He failed to complete the mission that God had ordered him to accomplish. He prophesied to the altar at Bethel and walked in mighty power in the eyes of the people. After he was out of the limelight he eased up and forgot the Word of the Lord. It is more important to follow God's instructions behind closed doors than it is in the eyes of the crowd. He did not finish his course and obey God to the end, and the spirit of death was transferred to his ministry.

AZAZEL

Though Azazel was the scapegoat in the Old Testament, this spirit manifested itself throughout the Bible. Demons do not die. When they are cast out they must go somewhere. In Matthew 8:28–34, the demons begged Jesus to allow them to go into the swine. This tells us two things:

1.   Demons are tormented if they are not sent to a certain place.
2.   We can direct demons where to go when we cast them out.

In the Old Testament it was the priest who sent the sins of the Israelites to Azazel in the wilderness. I have heard of people sending demons to the feet of Jesus. Personally, I have never really figured this one out. I have also heard some send demons to the pit or *Tartarus* (or *tartaroo*, a Greek word for *hell*). But I really think that it is interesting to see that the sins were sent into the wilderness to Azazel. Remember, the demons seek dry (wilderness) places even though they get no rest there.

Where do demons go after they are cast out of a person? The Book of Matthew says that they wander around in dry places seeking rest, but find none (Matt. 12:43). The word *dry* in the Greek is *anudros*, which means "a waterless place." Demons seek to escape to places that have no Spirit of God abiding in them. Even in dry places, demons still find no rest. In other words, though they seek dry places, they are still tormented in them and find no rest. You see, demons are dumb! They seek places where they know they will still be tormented. They are tormented in the desert. Demons are disembodied spirits, and they must have a warm body to reside in. The body must have life for them to exist, because the essence of a demon is to express himself. Demons need a body to "live through."

One night as my husband and I left an airport where we had flown into, we saw a dead body. The person had died in the car while traveling with his two children. He was lying on the side of the road when my husband and I arrived. I tried to raise the man from the dead until the rescue workers arrived. He was not breathing, but bubbles of mucus were coming from his nose and mouth.

The Lord revealed to me that this was the release of demons from the body. One of the children was mad and cursing because the rescue workers had taken so long to arrive. The other was painfully mourning the death of their father. I began to minister to the child who was mourning (in shock) the sudden death of their parent. This child accepted Jesus as Savior on the side of the road that night.

The other child did not want anything to do with God. He was cursing like a sailor as we prayed to God. It is not hard to figure out where the demons that left his father's body went. He willingly received them through his hard heart and foul mouth. Spirits are very comfortable in bloodlines. They like to stay in the family. This is where we get the phrase "generational curse." The term "familiar spirit" is also related to generational curses or "family demons."

We may as well "'fess up"! All of our families have specific demons. Even the medical society knows this. The first thing the doctor asks when a person gets a physical is what diseases did our family members incur. What the doctor is really doing is making *a checklist of the demons that run in our bloodline.*

The Bible says that these curses go back as far as four generations. Curses are manifestations of demonic interference. A curse is opposition against the blessings of God in our lives. The generational curses go back four generations, but the generational blessings go forward for one thousand. It is important to cut off the traffic of curses that transfer through our bloodline. Not only are we delivered when we overcome demonic infiltration in our lives, but our children's children are set free also.

Can a person with the Holy Spirit have a demon? The answer is unequivocally yes! The Holy Spirit resides in our spirit man, but demons live in the flesh. This is why witchcraft is a work of the flesh. James explains it well when he said that curses and blessing were coming out of the same mouth (James 3:10). Though he said it should not have been so, it was!

If a Christian can speak in tongues, then leave church and fornicate, a person with the Holy Spirit can have a demon. Jeremiah spoke of broken cisterns that could not hold water (Jer. 2:13). This is what it is like for a person who is trying to serve God but still lives a life of sin and gives entrance to demons. Such a person has "forsaken Me, the fountain of living waters" (Jer. 2:13).

Jeremiah asked the question, "Is Israel a servant? Is he a homeborn slave? Why is he spoiled?" (v. 14, KJV). The word *spoiled* is *baz* in the Hebrew, and it means "to become prey, booty or plunder." It means to be taken captive in the battle as a prize. When we are called to have dominion over the devil and we fall prey to his deceptions, we become a stone for the crown of satan. We become booty from the battle that he is proud to display as an open show against God.

> For it is impossible for those who were once enlightened, and have tasted the heavenly gift, and have become partakers of the Holy Spirit, and have tasted the good word of God and the powers of the age to come, if they fall away, to

renew them again to repentance, since they crucify again for themselves the Son of God, and *put Him to an open shame.*

—HEBREWS 6:4–6, EMPHASIS ADDED

This means that we can taste of the heavenly gifts and be partakers of the Holy Ghost and yet ultimately be cast out of the presence of God. What could make this possible? It is demonic infiltration of the soul. When the devil hijacks the mind (your soul), the body will follow!

Demons think of human bodies as their homes. They look for bodies that will suit their needs to exist. For example, a lust demon likes to abide in bodies that have done lustful acts before because this increases the demon's ability for more power in this area. Matthew 12:45 says that the spirits leave the body of a person and come back with seven spirits worse than those that left. In other words, a person who has been delivered from masturbation, yet returns to his sins, can now be open to the spirit of homosexuality.

When we are in right standing with God, a devil cannot infiltrate our coast. It is the name and the blood of Jesus that are a covering to us against transference of spirits. But we cannot operate in ways that oppose God and expect His hedge to protect us. Ecclesiastes reminds us that if we break a hedge, a serpent will bite us (Eccles. 10:8). The word *bite* means "to lend as usury on a loan." It refers to the interest of the bite.

When a snake bites a person, it is not the actual bite that kills the person. It is the poison that takes them out. When a person commits an act of sin, after the act is over, the interest of the act soaks in their soul like poison. Unforgiveness is a great example of the snakebite when a man breaks the hedge of God in his life. It is the most deceptive demon a person can ever deal with. The spirit of unforgiveness gives you a direct ticket to hell. This spirit will go to church with you, sing in the choir and even preach the gospel—and yet take you to hell.

Jesus said, "If you do not forgive, neither will your Father in heaven forgive your trespasses" (Mark 11:26). Unforgiveness is a type of spiritual cancer. It slowly eats away at the soul. It hides itself in the heart and consumes the soul. It is not that Jesus does not want to forgive us; He just cannot override the demon of unforgiveness that we have given "His place" in our hearts.

I have heard demonic spirits screaming out of people as they were being cast out, "I will just go to another body." I will never forget when my husband and I were ministering deliverance in a church in Colorado. We had sessions going on in several rooms. Demons began to cry out of one man, "Don't send us to the pit; please don't send us to the pit!" Then they asked us, "Send us to the people in the next room; they will gladly receive us there."

Demons can only go where they are welcomed and received. A person can have as many demons as he wants. But once we are delivered from spirits, we do not have to put up with them again. Once we are free indeed, we have the authority to be tormented no longer, but to become the tormentor.

God has given us power over all the power of the enemy! We must hold on to the beginning of our confidence until the end. The only ones who fell in the wilderness were those who sinned. All the children of Israel came out of Egypt, but not everyone was delivered from the wilderness. Our testimony must proceed past the bondage of Egypt; we must have victory over our wilderness situations. Though we all started in Egypt and are moving toward the promised land, we must go through the wilderness.

Many of the Israelites picked up the wrong attitude in the wilderness. Spirits of complaining and discontent plagued their hearts, and they became hard and cold in their belief toward God. The enemy wants to make our wilderness experience seem crueler than the Egypt out of which we have come. There are demons in the wilderness that are even more dangerous than the ones in Egypt. But we have more power in the wilderness that we had in Egypt.

"Where sin abounded, grace abounded much more" (Rom. 5:20). In Egypt, we only had "to sit," but in the wilderness, we are "sent." The wilderness represents the apostolic ministry of God. These are the weapons of our warfare, an apostolic life of hardship, but we have victory over it all! We can go through the wilderness and come out free!

The anointing is a repellent to spirits; it destroys the yoke. By the way, the anointing is transferable! Transference of spirits is the counterfeit of the release of God's anointing. One of the main ways that God releases His power to us is by the "laying on of hands." The woman with the issue of blood was healed when she touched the hem of Jesus' garment. The key word is contact. When she made contact with Jesus, the virtue went from Him to her.

The devil is a copycat. It is his desire to release his demonic virtue into our lives in any way possible so that God cannot use us. God releases His power to us so that He can use us for His glory. Transference of spirits is demonic, but transference of the Spirit is the will of God. God wants us to spread His gospel to the world.

The only way this can be done is by His Spirit. You do not have to walk around in fear. Just get full of God and release Him to someone else! There are many spirits in the land, but there is only one we should receive—the Holy Spirit.

Paul made sure the people understood what Jesus was preaching about. He said, "This Jesus whom I preach to you is the Christ" (Acts 17:3). In 2 Corinthians 11:4 we read, "For if he who comes preaches another Jesus whom we have not preached…you may well put up with it!" These verses refer to the simplicity of the gospel. Paul was telling the church at Corinth that he feared the possibility of deception creeping into the church. He used the example of the serpent that beguiled Eve through his subtlety. He told them to be watchful that their minds did not become corrupted for the simplicity of Christ. Discerning of spirits is needed more than ever in the body of

Christ. I believe that from the reading of Scripture we can be safe to say that there will be those who preach:

- Another Jesus spirit
- Another Holy Ghost
- Another gospel

These are counterfeit spirits on assignment to contaminate the seed of God. We have power over these spirits when we obey God. God told us to come out from among them, and He meant what He said! God is not mean. He just does not want us to pick up spirits that will hinder us from going forth. As believers, we can help prevent transference of spirits in several ways.

- Know them that you labor among (by the Spirit).

- Be anxious for nothing; do not be quick to let everybody lay hands on you.

- Present your body as an acceptable, living sacrifice unto God.

- If you know you are in sin (i.e., homosexuality, fornication, masturbation, backbiting, rebellion), do not lay hands on anyone until you get yourself together.

- Be led by the Spirit and listen to God as you walk with Him. We often get caught with hearing God only when we are in our closets. We need to be able to hear Him in our daily situations. "For as many as are led by the Spirit of God, these are sons of God" (Rom. 8:14). God is always speaking to us, but the devil is always countering God's Word by telling us that what we heard was our flesh. Do not be afraid; He will never leave or forsake us.

- God's grace is sufficient, and His mercy is new every morning. Even when we sometimes miss it, God will protect us. God commands us to walk in the Spirit.

This is not an easy thing to do, but with the "Helper" (the Holy Spirit) this can be achieved. On the other hand, when we haphazardly walk in God thinking that "it does not take all that," we neglect our part. The Holy Spirit "helps" us. This means that there is something that we have to do. When we do our part, all of heaven backs us up!

It will help you to realize that we are in a real war. This war cannot be seen with the physical eye. Spirits easily transfer in the midst of saints who have a "leisure club mentality." But when we develop a "warfare mentality," we understand that the weapons of our warfare are not carnal, but mighty through God to the pulling down of strongholds (2 Cor. 10:4).

Yes, I know about the power in the blood of Jesus. I know about putting on the whole armor of God. But if we disobey God, we make even these tools that God has given us null and void. What do I mean? For example, if God tells me not to get in a prayer line, I had better obey Him. No matter what it looks like, I have to adhere to the voice of God. I cannot stand in that prayer line and believe God to protect me if He has already instructed me not to go there. If I get in that line, I have crossed the bloodline. In essence, I would have left the will of God. The blood will not cover me until I repent and get in place. (See my book *From a Mess to a Miracle* for an in-depth teaching on sharpening your spiritual discerner.)

We can also take the initiative to "work out" our discerners by making ourselves very familiar with the Word of God. The Word makes us sharp in the spirit. People are not sensitive to the Spirit because their discerners have become dull. I believe it has a lot to do with what they have heard. Faith comes by hearing the Word of God. Our discerners are dulled through doubt. Doubt is contagious, and it can come through generational curses or even things you hear through the grapevine. No matter how it transfers, we must separate ourselves from it.

Consecration unto God is our greatest tool against the transference of spirits. Consecration is not a time you choose to fast and pray; *it is a LIFESTYLE!* Once you begin to live a consecrated lifestyle, you can go into the fiery furnace and come out without the smell of smoke on your clothes. You can be like Daniel, stand in the presence of the lions in the den and come out whole. It was not the power that the Hebrew boys had in the midst of their persecution that saved them—it was the lifestyle they had already lived.

Conclusion

I PRAY THAT THE information you have read in this book has blessed your soul. Jesus is coming back soon, and we do not need anything in our lives that will keep us from getting caught up. I do not know about you, but I want to meet Him in the sky. I believe in long life, but if anything happens and I die before Jesus returns, I want to see His face.

I was saved as the result of watching a movie called *A Thief in the Night*. If you have not accepted Jesus as Lord and Savior, this book could be the key that unlocks your destiny in Christ. Have you been born again? I am not talking about attending church services! Has Jesus entered into your life and made a difference? Taking it to the next level, have you fallen in love with Him?

There is no need to learn how to do warfare and deliverance if you do not have a solid relationship with God. Without a sure foundation (in Him), you will be like a broken cistern that has no ability to hold God's Spirit within. Thus you will forsake the fountain of living water (Jer. 2:13).

If you do not know Jesus and want to get to know Him, pray this prayer with me:

> *Father God, in the name of Jesus, I accept You into my heart. I believe that You died for my sins. I renounce every false god and idol that has taken up space in my life that You should occupy.*
>
> *Satan, I renounce you and all of your evil ways. Your wiles and devices shall no longer rule over my head. I*

renounce the prince of the power of the air. I withdraw my membership as a "child of disobedience," and I enroll as a "child of the King." I confess that I am a joint heir with Christ.

Every bondage that has gripped my soul up to this point in my life is on notice—Jesus is Lord forever! I submit to be delivered and filled with the Holy Ghost and to learn the principles of God so that I can please Him.

To Ministers and Deliverance Workers

It is my prayer that you will be a good steward of the information presented in this book. Deliverance ministry is the ministry of Jesus Christ, and we must protect it with everything on the inside of us. How can we do that? We can do this by operating in integrity, humility and love. Not only must we put on the whole armor of God to protect ourselves, but we must also put on the "new man" to protect the people with whom we deal on a daily basis.

When we put off the old man, we deal with the spirits of wrath, malice, blasphemy and filthy communication. But in putting on the new man, we use "renewed knowledge" after the image of Christ.

You see, we can walk in power in the midst of the multitudes, even raising the dead. But if we do not have the fruit of the Spirit operating in our lives, God is not pleased. The greatest test of the fruit of the Spirit happens in a person's life when he or she encounters opposition from opposing forces. It is easy to love when people flow with you, but the true test is when you can love those that oppose you on a consistent basis. Consistent enemies have brought true balance in my life. This balance keeps me from the religious ignorance of believing everybody is for me.

We should take comfort in the fact that there are more for us than against us, but we will always have those who are against us. In deliverance ministry you will incur enemies. The devil does not like to be cast out! He will retaliate, and he does it through people—most likely those who are closest to you. Deliverance ministry is not for crybabies or those who cannot take persecution. If you cannot stand to be talked about, you may as well throw your paper towels and buckets in right now!

People will attempt to scandalize your name. The good thing is that if you endure it with a right attitude, you will be victorious. When people come up against you because of who you are or what you are doing in Jesus, there is always a reward. At times you will want to have a "thank-you party" for tribulation. Enjoy it! Count it all joy! A miracle is just around the corner!

It is easy to praise God in the midst of tribulation when your mind is focused on where you are going and not on what you are going through. This kind of attitude pleases the Lord. And when we please God, even our enemies are at peace with us.

༺༻

I'm outta here!

—APOSTLE KIM

Appendix A

Combat Scriptures to Defeat Our Enemy

I N THIS SECTION I want to review some Scripture verses that teach us how we should pray in order to deal with this hard-core antagonist who is operating against us in the spirit. Remember, "the weapons of our warfare are not carnal [natural] but mighty in God for pulling down strongholds" (2 Cor. 10:4). We war not against flesh and blood but against spirit forces that are assigned to hold us down. As we study the scriptures and pray these prayers, get your mind off the natural realm, and get a revelation about who your enemies really are.

> Thy right hand, O LORD, is become glorious in power: thy right hand, O LORD, hath dashed in pieces the enemy. And in the greatness of thine excellency thou hast overthrown them that rose up against thee.
>
> —EXODUS 15:6–7, KJV

> *God, You said that You would be an enemy to our enemies and an adversary to our adversary.*

> And if you go to war in your land against the enemy that oppresseth you, then ye shall blow an alarm with the trumpets; and ye shall be remembered before the Lord your God, and ye shall be saved from your enemies.
>
> —NUMBERS 10:9, KJV

God, You said that if we go into war in our own land against the enemy that oppresses us, we should blow the trumpet, and we would be remembered before the Lord and saved from our enemies. Remember us as we battle our own enemies in our own land.

...wherewith thine enemy shall distress thee in thy gates.

—DEUTERONOMY 28:57, KJV

We bind the spirit whereby the enemy is trying to distress us in our own gates.

The eternal God is thy refuge, and underneath are the everlasting arms: and he shall thrust out the enemy from before thee; and shall say, Destroy them.

—DEUTERONOMY 33:27, KJV

Father, I thank You that You are my refuge and that You thrust out the enemy from before me. You are God, and You deliver our enemies into our hands.

And Saul was yet the more afraid of David; and Saul became David's enemy continually.

—1 SAMUEL 18:29, KJV

Father, I thank You that You have delivered me from my enemies, which are continually before me; I thank You that I have victory over my continual enemies.

Behold, I will deliver thine enemy into thine hand, that thou mayest do to him as it shall seem good unto thee.

—1 SAMUEL 24:4, KJV

Father, I praise You, and I thank You that after You have delivered our enemies into our hands, You allow us to do unto them as it seems good to us.

For if a man find his enemy, will he let him go well away?

Wherefore the LORD reward thee good for that thou hast done unto me this day.

—1 SAMUEL 24:19, KJV

Lord, strengthen me to release my enemies after they are captured, for Your Word says that if a man find his enemy and let him go, You will reward him good.

He delivered me from my strong enemy, and from them that hated me: for they were too strong for me.

—2 SAMUEL 22:18, KJV

Father, deliver me from my strong enemy and from them that hate us, for they are too strong for me. Father, You are my stay.

If there be in the land famine, if there be pestilence, blasting, mildew, locust, or if there be caterpiller; if their enemy besiege them in the land of their cities; whatsoever plague, whatsoever sickness there be…then hear thou in heaven… and give to every man according to his ways, whose heart thou knowest.

—1 KINGS 8:37–39, KJV

Father, deliver and keep me from the enemies of the land—famine, pestilence, blasting, mildew, locust, caterpillar, plague or sickness.

God shall make thee fall before the enemy: for God hath power to help, and to cast down.

—2 CHRONICLES 25:8, KJV

Father, You have the power to help and to cast down; help me not to fall before my enemies.

For I was ashamed to request of the king an escort of soldiers and horsemen to help us against the enemy on the road, because we had spoken to the king, saying, "The hand of our God is upon all those for good who seek Him, but His power and His wrath are against all those who forsake Him."

—EZRA 8:22

*God, help me against the enemy that would stand
"in the way."*

Then we departed from the river of Ahava on the twelfth
day of the first month, to do to Jerusalem. And the hand of
our God was upon us, and He delivered us from the hand
of the enemy and from ambush along the road.

—EZRA 8:31

*God, deliver me from the enemy of the Jews, the
ones who hate me because I belong to God.*

He tears me in His wrath, and hates me; He gnashes at me
with His teeth; my adversary sharpens His gaze on me. They
gape at me with their mouth, they strike me reproachfully
on the cheek, they gather together against me.

—JOB 16:9–10

*Father God, deliver me from the demonic manifes-
tations of my enemies.*

- *They tear me in their wrath.*
- *They hate me for no reason.*
- *They gnash me with their teeth.*
- *They sharpen their eyes upon me.*
- *They gape upon me with their mouth.*
- *They have smitten me on my cheek with
  reproach.*

Surely you have spoken in my hearing, and I have heard the
sound of your words, saying, "I am pure, without transgression; I am innocent, and there is no iniquity in me."

—JOB 33:8–9

*In the name of Jesus, I bind the spirit that would
make people find occasion against me even when I
am living right. I am not bound by those who have
made up their minds against me and count me as
an enemy. I am released from those who have tried
to put my feet in stocks and mark my paths.*

If I have repaid evil to him who was at peace with me,
Or have plundered my enemy without cause,
Let the enemy pursue me and overtake me.

—PSALM 7:4–5

Father, I repent if I have (knowingly or unknowingly) rewarded evil unto him who was at peace with me.

—

For You have maintained my right and my cause;
You sat on the throne judging in righteousness.
You have rebuked the nations,
You have destroyed the wicked;
You have blotted out their name forever and ever.

—PSALM 9:4–5

Father, I thank You that You have maintained my right and my cause. You have rebuked the heathen on my behalf and destroyed the wicked. You have put out their name forever. Destruction has come to a perpetual end, and the memorial of my enemies perish with them.

—

Consider and hear me, O LORD my God;
Enlighten my eyes,
Lest I sleep the sleep of death;
Lest my enemy say,
"I have prevailed against him";
Lest those who trouble me rejoice when I am moved.
But I have trusted in Your mercy;
My heart shall rejoice in Your salvation.

—PSALM 13:3–5

Jesus, I trust in Your mercy. I believe that my enemies will not say that they have prevailed against me. Those that trouble me will not rejoice, because I will not be moved.

—

[You] have not shut me up into the hand of the enemy;
You have set my feet in a wide place.

—PSALM 31:8

*Father, I thank You that You have not shut me up
into the hand of my enemies. You have set my feet
in a large room.*

—

By this I know that You are well pleased with me,
Because my enemy does not triumph over me.

—PSALM 41:11

*Father, I know that You have given me favor and
that my enemies cannot triumph over me.*

—

Because of the voice of him who reproaches and reviles,
Because of the enemy and the avenger.

—PSALM 44:16

*In the name of Jesus, I bind the voice of reproach
that comes by reason of the enemy and the avenger.*

—

For it is not an enemy who reproaches me;
Then I could bear it.
Nor is it one who hates me who has exalted himself against
me;
Then I could hide from him.

—PSALM 55:12

*Father, I thank You for delivering me from the
reproach of men considered to be my equal. I will not
be consumed by those who were close acquaintances.*

—

For You have been a shelter for me,
A strong tower from the enemy.

—PSALM 61:3

*Lord, I thank You that You shelter me as a strong
tower from my enemies. I will abide in Your taber-
nacle forever and trust in the cover of Your wings.*

—

Hear my voice, O God, in my meditation;
Preserve my life from fear of the enemy.
Hide me from the secret plots of the wicked,
From the rebellion of the workers of iniquity,
Who sharpen their tongue like a sword,
And bend their bows to shoot their arrows—bitter words,
That they may shoot in secret at the blameless;
Suddenly they shoot at him and do not fear.
They encourage themselves in an evil matter.
—Psalm 64:1–5

Father, in the name of Jesus:

- *Preserve my life from the fear of my enemy.*
- *Hide me from the "secret counsel" of the wicked.*
- *Protect me from the insurrection of workers of iniquity.*
- *Keep me from those who whet their tongues against me like a sword.*
- *Make me safe from those who bend their bows and shoot arrows of bitter words.*
- *Cover me from those who shoot at me in secret.*
- *Separate me from those who encourage themselves in evil matters.*

Lift up Your feet to the perpetual desolations.
The enemy has damaged everything in the sanctuary,
Your enemies roar in the midst of Your meeting place;
They set up their banners for signs.
—Psalm 74:3–4

Father, deliver me from the evil the enemy has done "in the sanctuary." I have victory over the "roars" of the enemy in the midst of the congregation. I bind up the ensigns that the enemy sets up as signs in the church.

O God, how long will the adversary reproach?
Will the enemy blaspheme Your name forever?
—Psalm 74:10

Father, deliver me from the reproach of my adver-
sary, and let him not blaspheme Your name forever.

Our fathers in Egypt did not understand Your wonders;
They did not remember the multitude of Your mercies,
But rebelled by the sea—the Red Sea.
Nevertheless He saved them for His name's sake,
That He might make His mighty power known.
He rebuked the Red Sea also, and it dried up;
So He led them through the depths
As through the wilderness.
He saved them from the hand of him who hated them,
And redeemed them from the hand of the enemy.

—PSALM 106:7–10

Father, I thank You...

- *That You saved me for Your name's sake that*
  Your mighty power might be known.
- *That You rebuked the Red Sea and caused it to*
  dry up.
- *That You led me through the depths and through*
  the wilderness.
- *That You saved me from them that hate me and*
  redeemed me from my enemy.

Let the redeemed of the LORD say so,
Whom He has redeemed from the hand of the enemy,
And gathered out of the lands,
From the east and from the west,
From the north and from the south.

—PSALM 107:2–3

Lord, You have gathered my enemies out of the
lands of the south, east, north and west.

For the enemy has persecuted my soul;
He has crushed my life to the ground;
He has made me dwell in darkness,
Like those who have long been dead,

Therefore my spirit is overwhelmed within me;
My heart within me is distressed.

—PSALM 143:3–4

*In the name of Jesus, I stand in the gap for those
that the enemy has smitten their life down to the
ground. I plead the blood of Jesus over those whom
the enemy has persecuted their souls. I prophesy
light to those whom the enemy has made to dwell in
darkness. Lord, have mercy on those who are overwhelmed within and are desolate at heart.*

Do not rejoice when your enemy falls,
And do not let your heart be glad when he stumbles.

—PROVERBS 24:17

*Father, I declare that I will not rejoice when my
enemies fall, and my heart will not be glad when
they stumble.*

If your enemy is hungry, give him bread to eat;
And if he is thirsty, give him water to drink;
For so you will heap coals of fire on his head,
And the LORD will reward you.

—PROVERBS 25:21–22

*Father, I have a revelation that if my enemies thirst,
I must give them water. If my enemies are hungry, I
must give them bread. If they mean evil against me,
my good deeds toward them will heaps coals of fire
upon their heads, and the Lord shall reward me.*

The north wind brings forth rain,
And a backbiting tongue an angry countenance.

—PROVERBS 25:23

*Lord, help me to present myself well and to abstain
from speaking negative things about others. Just as
the north wind drives the rain away, so does a backbiting tongue and an angry countenance.*

Faithful are the wounds of a friend,
But the kisses of an enemy are deceitful.

—PROVERBS 27:6

God, deliver me from the "kiss of death"! Faithful
are the wounds of a friend, but deceitful is the kiss
of an enemy.

So shall they fear
The name of the LORD from the west,
And His glory from the rising of the sun;
When the enemy comes in like a flood,
The Spirit of the LORD will lift up a standard against him.

—ISAIAH 59:19

God, I thank You that even when the enemy comes
in like a flood, You will raise a standard against him.

"I will scatter them as with an east wind before the enemy;
I will show them the back and not the face
In the day of their calamity."

Then they said, "Come and let us devise plans against
Jeremiah; for the law shall not perish from the priest, nor
counsel from the wise, not the word from the prophet.
Come and let us attack him with the tongue, and let us not
give heed to any of his words."

Give heed to me, O LORD,
And listen to the voice of those who contend with me!
Shall evil be repaid for good?
For they have dug a pit for my life.
Remember that I stood before You
To speak good for them,
To turn away Your wrath from them.
Therefore deliver up their children to the famine,
And pour out their blood
By the force of the sword;
Let their wives become widows
And bereaved of their children.
Let their men be put to death,

Their young men be slain
By the sword in battle.
Let a cry be heard from their houses,
When You bring a troop suddenly upon them;
For they have dug a pit to take me,
And hidden snares for my feet.
Yet, LORD, You know all their counsel
Which is against me, to slay me.
Provide no atonement for their iniquity,
Nor blot out their sin from Your sight;
But let them be overthrown before You.
Deal thus with them
In the time of Your anger.

—JEREMIAH 18:17–23

In the name of Jesus, I bind the spirits that try to smite the voice of the prophetic. The law shall not perish from the mouth of the priest. The counsel shall not leave the wise. The word shall not be taken from the mouth of the prophet. They that smite the prophet with the tongue shall not prosper. The word of the prophet shall not be ignored. God, I thank You that You have heard the voice of the enemy against Your anointed.

When my enemy has dug a pit for me, remember how I stood before You and spoke well of them. Because of this, Lord, deliver their children to famine, pour out their blood by force of the sword, let their wives be bereaved of their children and be widows, let their men be put to death, and let their young men be slain by the sword in battle. Let a cry be heard from their houses when You shall suddenly bring a troop upon them.

Yes, they have dug a pit to take me, and have hidden snares under my feet. Lord, reveal the counsel that is working against me to slay me. Forgive not their iniquity, and do not blot out their sins from Your sight. Let my enemies be overthrown before You. Lord, deal with them when You are mad.

Another parable He put forth to them, saying: "The kingdom of heaven is like a man who sowed good seed in his field; but while men slept, his enemy came and sowed tares among the wheat and went his way."

—MATTHEW 13:24–25

In the name of Jesus, I bind the enemy that would sow tares among the wheat.

Behold, I give you the authority to trample on serpents and scorpions, and over all the power of the enemy, and nothing shall by any means hurt you.

—LUKE 10:19

Jesus, I thank You that I have power over all the power of my enemy.

Paul, filled with the Holy Spirit, looked intently at him and said, "O full of all deceit and all fraud, you son of the devil, you enemy of all righteousness, will you not cease perverting the straight ways of the Lord?"

—ACTS 13:9–10

I bind the "enemy of righteousness."

The last enemy that will be destroyed is death.

—1 CORINTHIANS 15:26

In the name of Jesus, I come up against the "last enemy" (the enemy of death).

Appendix B

Warfare Terms

Ahab spirit—the spirit that comes upon leadership to cause them to walk in the ways of the ungodly and to turn the hearts of the people toward idolatry. This spirit not only puts up with Jezebel, but also is in total agreement and works with the Jezebel spirit.

antichrist—any spirit that is antagonistic against the Word or the things of God

astral projection—when the gross (physical) body lies dormant and the astral (spirit) body travels or is supernaturally projected. This state takes place through a mediumistic trance; the astral body is a type of ectoplasm (a various luminous substance) that emanates from the body of the traveler. The ectoplasm is considered by spiritualists to be the materialization of the astral body.

Azazel—the scapegoat demon of the desert. This is the spirit to which Aaron transferred the sins of the people on the Day of Atonement. Azazel is the strongman for transference of spirits.

battering ram—tool by which stubborn spirits are dealt with in warfare. These spirits must be commandeered, and the doors must be kicked in (Ezek. 4:2).

beguiling spirit—to mislead by deception; to deprive or cheat; to misrepresent on purpose

black magic—magic sent forth for evil purposes; ultimately effective by the conjuring up of demons

blocking spirit—a stymie or hindering spirit placed in the direct path of the purpose of God to frustrate, irritate or to make difficult

bewitchment—to be under the power or influence of, by the casting of an evil spell or illness; to be under the power of the Wicca (witch) through fascination; closely related to enchantment. Enchantment is the act, but bewitchment is the effect of the act on a person.

candle magic—magic by the use of candles with the use of colors for special outcome; usually used with incantations (example: mind-blinding candle)

cantrip—a witch's trick; called "Hocus Pocus" in Great Britain; a cloak of deception or a sleight of the hand

cauterize—to kill a spirit to the root and take its ability to rise again (Nah. 1:9)

chant—to repeat a series of syllables or words monotonously

celestial high places—the place where demonic activity operates in the second heaven

contagious magic—magic based on the belief that things that have once been in contact continue to have an influence on each other after their separation. It is believed that performing the rites of black magic over strings of hair, fingernails and other personal belongings can harm a person.

The act of cursing objects is called fetishism, whereby spirits are assigned and attached to objects, articles of clothing and the like. Everything God has on the light side the devil has a counterfeit for on the dark side. Paul sent the anointing on cloths to heal and deliver; likewise, satan does the same to curse.

death spirit—physical or spiritual death in relationship to man. It came into existence through disobedience in the Garden of Eden.

diva—a woman that is worshiped; a goddess. This is a demonic term and is short for divination. Women of God should not be called divas.

eavesdropper spirits—a type of familiar spirit; operates through clairaudience (the psychic ability to hear)

ectoplasm—an invisible substance that appears slightly luminous and usually in a crystal or glistering form; denotes the presence of a disembodied spirit through astral projection. The significance is physical manifestation to the naked eye; it looks like the men on *Star Trek* when they were being beamed from one place to another.

enchantment—to greatly charm through deceptive or counterfeit power; used by magicians through imagery and magnification

exousia—the power spirits of the demonic rank. They are the FBI and CIA of the demons. They make things happen when everything else fails. All front-line soldiers must be prepared to stand against an *exousia* attack. This is the counterfeit of the *exousia* power of God.

fascination—to be infatuated or overly concerned about the things of the dark side. We should never go on spiritual excursions to the dark side. The Holy Spirit should bring the revelation to us. Occult material and books must be used with great discretion and covered with the blood of Jesus. God did not call us to be obsessed with a passion for knowing about the demonic. He does not want us to be ignorant of satan's devices and wiles, but our focus must be on Jesus. He is the author and finisher of our faith. To be tied up in any of the things mentioned in this definition is a spirit of "demonic fascination," and it must be broken.

faultfinding spirit—to seek a scapegoat in another person, place or thing; to send sins or faults to another's blame

first heaven—the heaven that includes what we can see in the physical (sun, moon, stars)

guile—craftiness; slyness; cunning; taking on the character of satan when dealing in business and other matters

gyromancy—the spirit of this age. It represents delirium and looks like a hurricane. Its form is the exact replica of the vortexes of hell.

hex—a spell that is to bring on misfortune or to cause failure in every area

hupsistos—the highest of heavens; most high heaven.

hupsoma—high or elevated person, place or thing; that which exalts itself against the knowledge of God (2 Cor. 10:5)

hupsos—sky; the upper atmosphere that arches over the earth

ideation—a fixed idea or obsession

imagery—the production of mental images or sounds through erroneous perception arising from misrepresentation; closely related to hallucination that is mental wandering. The foundation of curses sent by witchcraft against the born-again believer is imagery. It is only real if we receive it to be so. Jesus really has all power, and satan has to operate on a counterfeit authority. The devil has been stripped of all power, and it has been given to us.

incantation—phrases or formulas spoken, sung or chanted as a ritual to send curses

invocation—the calling forth of demons

Jezebel—a spirit that operates by "absolute power." Control and manipulation are its foundation; all that was left of Jezebel after the dogs devoured her were three body parts:

    Hands—to stop the work

Feet—to lead the steps

Head—to control the mind

judgment of witches and warlocks—the sentencing and ordering of witches and warlocks against the steps of God's people

kosmokrator—the gods of this world; the forces that cosmetically beautify the demonic to attract the soul. The biblical term is "the rulers of the darkness of this world."

ligature—a binding together of a tie or cord. Demons usually operate in groups of three. Ecclesiastes 4:12 says, "A threefold cord is not quickly broken."

lucky—a superstitious term used by the ungodly. There is no such thing as "luck" in Christ. We are either cursed or blessed; things do not just haphazardly happen to us. This term is an abomination for a saint to use and should be abolished from our vocabulary in reference to good things happening to us. All good things come from above and have nothing to do with luck.

magnification—to make something appear greater than what it really is. When Lucifer rebelled against God, he declared, "I will exalt my throne above the stars of God and above the height of the clouds. I will be like the Most High God." Since that time, he has roamed around like a roaring lion. He comes in like a flood, trying to raise his status and to heighten and intensify his power at any cost. The spirit of magnification puts a magnifying glass on him. In the end God will remove this magnifying glass as the Scripture tells. Kings will ask, "Is this the man?"

mental locution—words spoken to the mind in a strategic style for a specific purpose

natural man—the name occultists use for people who are "deceived by the physical senses" (especially saints). They are prey to erroneous beliefs and are not immune to physical disease of the flesh; they can only "walk" by what they see. First Corinthians 2:14 states that the natural man cannot receive the things of the Spirit.

nature spirit—spirits that cause man to inherit a dependency on the power of nature. Almost all ancient gods were personified powers of nature. Witches pray and sacrifice to the gods of the earth, wind, fire and water.

nimbus—a false glory or halo. Halos are demonic and unscriptural. Nimbus is the name of Harry Potter's broom.

omen—a thing or event regarded as a sign of future good or bad luck

potion magic—liquids, oils and potions used to cast spells. A popular oil to make someone leave their wife, or some such thing, is "Come to Me Oil." The person that is working the curse wears the oil, and it is supposed to attract the victim that is being baited.

poneria—the Greek word for wicked; to deteriorate or degenerate. This is the strongman of backsliding. This is the term used when a person's state is seven times worse through continual backsliding. Matthew 12:45 refers to the person who has received seven more spirits as a part of the "wicked" generation. The word *wicked* is *poneria* in the Greek.

ritual—a service or worship to a strongly believed observance; rites, rules or formalities of organized groups

ruler spirit—kosmokrator or world ruler; comes in direct contact with individuals, families, neighborhoods based on territorial assignment

scanner spirits—spies that travel and transport information through demonic ranks; reconnaissance and exploratory spirits

second heaven—the abode of the prince of the power of the air; positioned between the first and third heavens

self-inflicting curse through negative confession—words spoken out of the will of God that cause life-threatening results to the individual who has spoken them

spell—to charm or capture the mind to the point of enchantment or fascination, to blind or distract from the truth

spermatic word—a creative force of the spoken word that releases seed to reproduce; a word that contains life; the same as a "seeding"

spirit of Balaam—the spirit of the false prophet, especially concerning soothsaying gain

spirit of Cain—the spirit that causes God's people to kill their brothers and sisters as a result of greed, jealousy and stinginess

spirit of confusion—a spirit that causes bewilderment and cloudiness so that the truth is not made clear

spirit of divination—a soothsaying spirit that gives a person supernatural ability to know things about the past, present and future by demonic influence

spirit of Korah—spirit that causes rebellion against leadership with the ultimate goal of mass mutiny

spirit of litigation—an argumentative spirit that usually has to have the last word or to prove a point; easily drawn to legal battles

spirit of superstition—any belief, practice or rite that depends on magic, chance or dogma. To believe in luck is superstitious. Making a wish with birthday candles or throwing coins into a "wishing well" is superstitious and rooted in the demonic.

spirit of the wizard—an exceptionally gifted or chief witch; very clever and a master craftsman

stronghold—a spiritual place of bondage. Physical places can become spiritual strongholds, or a person can simply be garrisoned in their mind.

strongman—garrisons the stronghold; may not be the most powerful spirit, but is the gatekeeper or the controller of demonic traffic. His power is in his position.

terrestrial high places—high places men build in the earth realm. Hezekiah tore down the high places (*Nehushtan*, 2 Kings 18:4).

third eye—the spiritual avenue by which divinators see into the spirit realm. Through demonic infiltration, satan opens a third eye in the spirit realm to allow them to see what they cannot see with their natural eyes. In the spirit, this eye is placed in the middle of the forehead of the person. Some witches and warlocks have been known to tattoo an eye on their foreheads. This eye is closely related to the "all-seeing eye" on the dollar bill, which is the same eye that is the symbol of the Masonic lodges. Both of these demonic representations of "knowing" are very deceptive to the user. Even though they have power and can see some things, only God is omniscient. In doing warfare against this type of darkness, we must *blind the third eye*. In the natural realm, people are considered to have a sixth sense or extrasensory perception. This is called *clairsentience* in the occult arena, and indicates psychic sensitivity (the peculiar feeling that something is about to happen, a "hunch"). The only way we should supernaturally know things is by the Holy Spirit. Any other avenue is demonic.

third heaven—where the Most High God resides; the heaven of heavens; throne room

threefold cord—a spiritual bonding that causes a tying together of spiritual unity. Once unified, this grouping is not quickly broken. This term can refer to that which is of God or the demonic.

vain imagination—thoughts that are senseless, futile and have no use by God. We have to be watchful not to think things that are idle and going toward a dead end. They entice an external debate with internal consideration of that which exalts itself against the knowledge of God. This is wasted imagination. Our imagination was given to us to meditate on God and His purposes. This frame of mind makes an idol of human reasoning and ultimately leads to spiritual death. God destroyed all of mankind for the imaginations of men.

vex—to irritate; to inflict or agitate in a petty or nagging way

vortex—openings that lead from hell to the earth (usually strategically set near fault lines). Demons are dispatched through these gateways to do satan's bidding in the earth. See gyromancy.

warring spirit—an instigating spirit that incites antagonism between parties to cause a breach in friendly relationships

watcher spirits—guard specified areas; stationary informants that send information to higher-ranking demons by scanner spirits. Their goal is to maintain territory and not be moved at any cost.

white magic—magic that is thought to be positive or to work on a person's behalf (There is none!)

wile—a beguiling trick of the enemy

witchcraft spirits—spirits of rebellion that cause a person to operate in a power outside the realm of the true and living God. Witchcraft works fluently through dirty hearts. The sixth chapter of Proverbs lists seven things God hates. One of them is a heart that manufactures wickedness. David prayed that God would give him a clean heart and renew in him a right spirit.

witching hour—a demonic watch set aside by witches and warlocks to send curses to victims, usually midnight to 3:00 a.m.

Xanadu—a place of idolatry

Notes

CHAPTER 1
THE NEW BIRTH

1. *Against All Odds* was self-published in 2000 and is available from Spread the Word Publishing, P. O. Box 40278, Jacksonville, Florida 32203-0278. *From a Mess to a Miracle* was published by Creation House Press, Lake Mary, Florida, in 2002.

CHAPTER 3
WHO IS THE STRONGMAN?

1. Kimberly Daniels, *From a Mess to a Miracle* (Lake Mary, FL: Creation House Press, 2002).
2. Ibid.

CHAPTER 4
DEALING WITH THE SPIRIT OF MAGNIFICATION

1. If you do not know much about apostolic ministry I recommend that you read Apostle John Eckhardt's book, *Leadershift* (Chicago, IL: Crusaders Ministries, 2000). I would also recommend *Spheres of Authority* by C. Peter Wagner (Colorado Springs, CO: Global Harvest, 2002).

CHAPTER 8
DELIVERANCE TESTIMONIES

1. Kimberly Daniels, *Against All Odds* (Jacksonville, FL: Spread the Word Publishing, 2000).

TAPES ON DELIVERANCE BY KIMBERLY DANIELS

Family Warfare	6 tapes	$30.00
Mental Disorders	4 tapes	$20.00
High Places	6 tapes	$30.00
The Strongman	2 tapes	$10.00
Warfare Prayers	2 tapes	$10.00
Warfare Update	3 tapes	$15.00
Warfare in Relationships	4 tapes	$20.00
Discerning Spirits	3 tapes	$15.00
Animal Spirits	3 tapes	$15.00
Come Out!	2 tapes	$10.00
East Coast Warfare 2002	6 tapes	$30.00
Inner City Deliverance	Video	$15.00
Culture Worship	Video	$15.00
Advanced Deliverance	3 tapes	$15.00
Spiritual Warfare 2000	4 tapes	$20.00
The Spirit of the World	2 tapes	$10.00

OTHER BOOKS BY KIMBERLY DANIELS

Against All Odds
From a Mess to a Miracle
3-D (Deliverance, Dominion and Divination) Warfare Manual

To order tapes or books, or for further information,
please contact:

Spoken Word Ministries
Apostle Kimberly Daniels
P. O. Box 40278
Jacksonville, FL 32203-0278

Phone: (904) 357-3500
Fax: (904) 598-1412

E-mail:
apostlekd@bustadevil.com

Website:
www.kimberlydaniels.com

For information about Christian education, contact
Word Bible College by e-mail: wbc@bustadevil.com.